THE GREAT MISSION OF

JESUS CHRIST

ON EARTH

THE GREAT MISSION OF

JESUS CHRIST

ON EARTH

John Entsuah

ARPress

ILLUMINATING IDEAS
EMPOWERING VOICES

ARPress
45 Dan Road Suite 5
Canton MA 02021

Hotline: 1(888) 821-0229
Fax: 1(508) 545-7580

Ordering Information:
Quantity sales. Special discounts are available on quantity purchases by corporations, associations, and others. For details, contact the publisher at the address above.

Printed in the United States of America.
ISBN-13:   Paperback   979-8-89330-554-8
               eBook   979-8-89330-555-5

Library of Congress Control Number: 2024901071

Dedication

This book is dedicated to my God parent, my Father/Mother God. And my elder brother Jesus, the first Christ, the first born son, and to all my Christed brothers and sisters in heaven who are earnestly waiting for our return to our celestial home to meet our God parent. And to the light workers on earth who are busily trying to shift the Christians and humanity from their human consciousness of separation from God to their Christ consciousness of oneness with God through prayer, meditation and fasting to connect directly with Jesus Christ to receive the Holy Spirit and the light of Christ for the activation of their Christ consciousness to enable them to enter into the kingdom of God.

CONTENTS

Acknowledgments

To my lovely wife, Christina—I want to thank you for all your love and support. I also want to thank my children—Amethyst, Zadkiel, Ella and Ezekiel for being such wonderful children… And special thanks to my daughter Ella who helped to typed my manuscript.

To the staff of Christian Faith Publishing Inc, who put the book, The great mission of Jesus Christ on earth to make it possible .

My deepest appreciation and my heart-felt thanks goes to all of you.

Preface

The hidden teaching of Jesus Christ is also known as the spiritual gospel of Jesus Christ. Most of these teachings were hidden or suppressed by the early Christians during the Roman empire when Constantine became the emperor and took control over all the churches and organized them into one body. He organized a conference of all the church leaders to formulate one church doctrine to unite them. It was during this conference of the church leaders that many advance spiritual gospels of Jesus Christ were removed and suppressed or rejected by the opposing sides and then created the Apostle's Creed. The rejected advance spiritual gospel of Jesus Christ was kept hidden for over a thousand years.

Now the most advance spiritual gospel of Jesus Christ is out in full force to change the earth and humanity—from human consciousness life of separation from God to Christ consciousness life of oneness with God.

This is the message of Jesus Christ to us and all the Christians now.

My Spiritual Experience and Encounter with the Lord Jesus Christ

Through intuitive direction, I learned that prayer, meditation, and fasting are the greatest tools that our God-Parent has given us to use to crawl our way back to Him. *Prayer* is talking to God, transmitting energy to God, which contains what you want from God. *Meditation* is intuitive listening to God within your soul with your inner ears to receive energy from God, which contains your desires. *Fasting* prepares your body and your soul by removing all the restraining forces and spiritual blocks, from your soul and body so that the Holy Spirit energy can flow freely from God into your heart to communicate.

With this in mind, I devoted much time to prayer, meditation, and fasting. I prayed and asked Jesus Christ to open my spiritual eyes that I might be able see him and my spiritual ears that I might be able to hear him so that I might become a better and more perfect instrument for his great and glorious work on earth.

Then one day, as I was in a meditative state, I felt a quickening movement in my heart. It was a soft, sweet feeling of joy that spread throughout my entire body, as if an invisible water or energy had poured over me. It penetrated my core and every cell of my being. It gave me a sweet joy and a sense of inner knowledge that my prayers had been fulfilled by the Lord Jesus Christ.

The next intuitive direction was constant prayer, meditation, and fasting. Dreams were also continual. Every night's sleep was as if I was putting my physical body down and going to another world to receive training. I would wake up in the morning and know what to do. Sometimes I would know which of the psalms to read as my prayer and message from the Lord Jesus Christ.

This meditative intuitive experience taught me that my heart is the teacher and my mind is the student. The student must always communicate with the teacher to learn and practice. It made it clear to me that the heart is the shepherd and the mind is the sheep; the sheep must always submit to the good shepherd for divine guidance and protection in order to reach its destination. This is the foundation of my life.

It taught me again that my heart is connected to heaven while my mind is connected to earth and that there must be direct, open communication between the two before heaven can change the earth. The communication between the heart and the mind is the key to raising my spiritual energy to transform myself to be able to see and hear Jesus Christ. Jesus is a high-energy being, and the only way to be able to see and hear him is to raise my spiritual energy in my body, soul, and spirit through prayer, meditation, and fasting.

How do I see him? Our brain is a communication system created by God. Inside our head, behind our eyes, is a spiritual-energy information receiver similar to that of our cell phone or television; both can receive and transmit pictures and sound. The three most important things that I knew to do intuitively were constant prayer, meditation, and fasting, as well as washing my body in the ocean every week. As I continued to fast, pray, meditate, and wash in the ocean, the energy in my heart intensified; that is, it increased and expanded and started to push the spiritual darkness from my soul and body. With my eyes closed, I saw the spiritual darkness behind my eyes began to lighten and finally became like a television screen. It was as if my mind or brain was now being in tune with some heavenly broadcasting station and receiving programs that forecast my future and the future of humanity. The screen became white and transparent like a crystal liquid water, so clean. In the center of the screen was a small white arrow, constantly spinning and creating pictures that gave me information and visions of what is to come both in my personal life and on the planet. I compare this small arrow with the small cursor on the computer screen. It is interesting to observe that the human brain can function like a television, capable of communicating with some heavenly station or a divine being like Jesus Christ.

In my vision, I saw an American flag. I saw myself traveling to America by plane. I saw the schools and colleges that I would be attending, the places I would be working, and religious institutions that I would be joining. I saw war, which I can now interpret as the Gulf War, during which President George W. Bush Jr. and his NATO Allies fought with Saddam Hussein. I saw armed Muslims in faceto-face confrontation with the well-armed soldiers of NATO. I saw hundreds of rockets and bombs frying in the skies. I saw tanks and planes, jet fighters and helicopters. There were killings and destruction and a great dark smoke. I am now certain that the smoke was caused by the oil wells blown up by the Iraqi forces in Kuwait. I saw myself working on a ship and traveling from one country to another.

There were other visions pertaining to myself and the planet that I will not discuss here, but I will talk about it at a later time. The most important thing for you to understand is that, God has the answer to every question, the solution to every problem. All you need to do is to establish your communication link with him. Communication between heaven and earth is the key to changing the earth into a celestial planet.

Constant prayer, meditation, fasting, and washing were the key factors. Through intuitive knowledge and direction, I washed myself in the ocean at least once a week. For some mysterious reasons, the ocean water had some cleansing properties that affected my body. And so by combining it with prayer meditation fasting and washing, I felt really good.

I discovered that the cleansing process must take place internally as well as externally. During meditation, my energy level was raised to allow internal cleansing as well as increase my overall energy level. As I bathed, I gain energy from the ocean for external or bodily cleansing.

This quickly revealed to me the reason Jesus said, "Except a man be born again of water and of the Holy Spirit he cannot enter into the kingdom of God," (John 3:5).

John the Baptist said, "I baptize with water unto repentance, but He that comes after me baptizes with the Holy Spirit and with Fire," (Matthew 3:11). This showed me that water and fire work hand in hand when it comes to cleansing and creativity. John the Baptist came to provide baptism by water for the cleansing and preparation of your body. Jesus Christ also came to give you the fire baptism of the heart for internal cleansing to raise your energy and remove the spiritual darkness and opening up your spiritual eyes and ears. He did this so that you might be able to see and hear him and also be able to communicate with the citizens of heaven and receive divine directions for your own personal life, as well as learn how to teach others to do the same.

Remember that water baptism and fire baptism must be done every day or every week. You must meditate daily to draw the Holy Spirit energy from Jesus Christ and the universal Christ to feed the Christ fire in your heart to grow. You must also wash in the ocean or saltwater to cleanse your body every day or every week. This is what I did to achieve this result.

There came a time that I felt that I have triggered an unknown world within myself that I couldn't escape. But the divine hand was at work; although I was in pain, I was urged to keep going because victory and true happiness awaited me in this life as well as eternally. This suffering was but a moment and that I should not worry; all would be fine in the future. Now I stand victorious.

In my vision, I saw the colors of the rainbow within myself. The future of humanity and the planet is bright, but they will never reach the height without challenge. Ignorance is the enemy creating misunderstanding, war, and hostility and taking away peace. This retards humanity's progress. Knowledge is power that enlightens humanity's progress and establishes peace. Therefore, we must open our hearts and minds and be willing to learn new things, discovering what the universe is all about and how we fit into the universal plan of God.

In my vision, I saw the rainbow within myself. It is amazing to see that the true nature of who we really are is being of light energy clothed with physical body, soul, and spirit, and this light energy breaks into spectrum of colors. The light energy creates the consciousness in us, and out of the consciousness comes the creative concepts of God that want to be expressed through our physical bodies. Our bodies then serve as vehicles of expression.

The creative concepts of God are high-energy concepts that exist inside the high-energy consciousness. This consciousness is called Christ consciousness, the priesthood power. The creative concepts that exist inside the Christ consciousness are the celestial or divine science and technology, with which all the celestial star systems were created, and the holy light universe were formed. Out of the same divine celestial science and technology came the natural science and technology, with which we create our ships, airplanes, telephones, radios, computers, communication systems, cell phones, and television systems.

Have you wondered why Jesus, a high-energy being with Christ consciousness, was able to walk on the sea? He was using the divine celestial science and technology, which is much more powerful than our own natural science and technology. He used this for his transfiguration. He used it to heal the sick and raise the dead. He used it to defeat death on the cross and make his ascension into the high-energy world, heaven. With divine celestial science and technology, you can override the natural world of pain, sin, disease, and death and transform it into a high-energy world of peace, creativity, adventure, love, harmony, beauty, and eternal life in the presence of God.

This is the message of Jesus Christ. He wants us to give up our human consciousness for Christ consciousness, which will give us the divine celestial science and technology needed to change our world for the better, a world where love reigns in the heart, a world of beauty, and celestial music of peace.

My inner teacher teaches me these things; therefore, I urge you to go within yourself through meditation, prayer, and fasting to connect with your inner teacher, the Christ. Free yourself from the grip of low-energy human consciousness, and achieve the high-energy Christ consciousness now, also called the priesthood power of Christ. God is the author of my life; therefore, I owe to him strict conformity to his divine plan for me and for the universe. That is common sense; I need not to be persuaded by anybody. Why? Because I have found Christ within myself and in my heart; the kingdom of God is within me.

What about you? Have you found him, or do you go to church every Sunday to listen to a sermon about how nice Jesus is without learning how to connect with him in your heart through meditation, prayer, and fasting? This is the challenge you need to conquer to be able to step into the kingdom of God within yourself. When you answer this question, you will find the kingdom of God.

Why do you have to go to church to find a kingdom that you already have within yourself? I'm not saying that you shouldn't go to church, but your spiritual common sense should tell you where to find the kingdom of God—your heart. Meditation is the key. The mind holds the key to the heart. In meditation, you bring your mind in tune with your heart and step into the secret chamber of the heart of your soul. Here, you will find Christ as a light being sitting upon the mercy seat, ready to respond to all of your needs. This Christ in your heart is the godly part of you that you need to contact every day. He sits upon the throne of the kingdom of God within you.

This is what is missing in some of the Christian churches today, and it needs to be restored. This is what Satan has taken away from them, unbeknown to them, because he knows that the day that you are able to contact your Christ Power and Jesus Christ in the heart of your soul, he will not stand a chance. You will defeat him.

Thank you, and the peace of the Lord be with you.

John Entsuah

Advance Hidden Spiritual Teachings of Jesus Christ

The spiritual gospel begins with our God-Parent in heaven known as the Alpha and Omega, also known as I AM THAT I AM who introduced himself to Moses in the burning bush in the wilderness in Pharaoh's time in Egypt. The whole creation came from this one source—the Father/Mother God known as the I AM THAT I AM.

The divine Father and the divine Mother came together to make divine love to give birth to the divine man-child called the Christ. The first Christ, the only begotten Son of the Father/Mother God, the divine love full of grace and truth, as the Word of God, and through him the universal Holy Spirit and the Christ light energy came into being and gave birth to the whole creation. We are all Christed children of this supreme holy family of the universe.

> He was in the world and the world was made Him, and the world knew Him not, He came unto His own, and His own receive Him not, but as many as receive Him, to them gave the power to become the sons of God, even to them that believe on His name: Which were born, not of the blood, nor of the will of the flesh, nor of the of man, but of God. (John 1:10–13)

The universal Christ light is individualize and personified in the heart of every soul on earth with consciousness by God and Jesus

Christ. Therefore, our point of contact with God and Jesus Christ is through the heart of our souls, "Christ in you the hope of glory" (Colossians 1: 27)

We must learn how to use meditation to enter into the heart of our souls to connect with the Light of Christ in our hearts, to link us with Jesus Christ and God to communicate with them to receive divine directions to guide our lives.

The Spiritual Fall from the Presence of God

Some of the Christed children fell spiritually from the presence of the God-Parent and lost contact with the Father/Mother God.

The spiritual fall began with Adam and Eve's disobedience to God's commandment not to eat the forbidden fruit in the garden of Eden according to the Bible.

Satan, the evil one, known as Lucifer, the prince of darkness of sin and death who had already fallen from the presence of God, came to tempt Adam and Eve to eat the forbidden fruit and cause their spiritual fall and eventually lost contact with God.

Who is Satan? Satan is originally known as Lucifer the Morning Star. He was one of the created beings by God. He was perfect and continued to remain perfect in his way until iniquity was found in him (Ezekiel 28:15b).

What was this iniquity? Ezekiel 28:17 says, "Your heart became proud on account of your beauty, and you corrupted your wisdom because of your splendor."

Lucifer became impressed with his own transcendent beauty, intelligence, power, and position and began to desire for himself in his heart the honor and glory that belongs to God alone.

The sin that corrupted Lucifer was self-generated pride and arrogance, and so Lucifer conceived evil in his heart and gave birth to himself as Satan. Therefore, whatever you conceive in your heart you give birth to it. This is absolute truth.

How are you falling from heaven, Oh Lucifer son of the morning! how are you cut down to the ground, who did weakens the nations. You said in your heart. I will ascend above the stars of God. I will set my throne on high, I will sit on the mount of assembly in the far reaches of the north. I will ascend above the height of the clouds. I will make myself like the most high, yet you shall be brought down to hell, to the sides of the pit. (Isaiah 14:12–15)

And there was war in heaven: Michael and his angels fought against the dragon; and the dragon fought and his angels, and prevail not; neither was their place found any more in heaven. And the great dragon was cast out that old serpent, call the devil and Satan which deceive the whole world: he was cast out into the earth, and his angels were cast out with him. (Revelation 12:7–9)

And I heard a loud voice saying in heaven. Now is come salvation and strength, and the kingdom of God and the power of Christ: for the accuser of our brethren is cast down, which accused them before our God day and night. And they overcame him by the blood of the lamb, and by the word of their testimony; and they loved not their lives unto death. (Revelation 12:10–12)

The Fall of Lucifer from the Spiritual Light of God in Heaven to the Spiritual Darkness

Revelation 12:4 says, "Satan was cast down to earth with one third of the heavenly angels who chose to follow him, by Arch Angel Michael and his legions of light." By God's order.

The one-third of the heavenly angels who chose to follow Satan became legions of darkness and antichrist on earth. And two-thirds of the heavenly angels who chose to follow Jesus Christ are the legion of light and Christ consciousness, who assist humanity to make their shift from human consciousness of separation from God to Christ consciousness of oneness with God.

Lucifer, after his spiritual fall from heaven to earth, is now known as Satan or the devil, the prince of darkness, death, and hell. His main goal is to take over the earth and the human race for himself through sin, lies, confusion, and spiritual darkness to create his own kingdom of darkness with his one-third of the fallen angels.

Lucifer's first goal on earth was to tempt Eve to get to Adam.

> Lucifer asked Eve, what did God say? And Eve replied, God said, of every tree in the garden you can freely eat, but the tree of knowledge of good and evil you shall not eat it, for the day that you eat it you shall surely die nevertheless you have your free will. Lucifer replied. You will not surely die you too will become Like God knowing good and evil." (Genesis 2:16–17, 3:1)

So Eve was convinced to eat the forbidden fruit and gave a portion to Adam to eat. This was disobedience to God's commandment and resulted to their spiritual fall (Genesis 3:1–7).

Originally, Adam and Eve were beings of light, there was no darkness in them, and the only thing they knew was good. They had a sense of innocence and light. They knew nothing about sin, darkness, evil, and death. They were God's children of light with no experience of evil, sin, darkness, and death. Lucifer knew and took advantage of that and caused the spiritual of fall of Adam and Eve, which resulted in their spiritual death first and by their physical death later.

We, the human race, as descendants of Adam and Eve, inherited this spiritual fall—a disconnection from our God-Parent. So today we all have a veil of spiritual darkness of sin and death within our souls, which we inherited from Adam and Eve. This has disconnected us from God, and it has to be removed by Jesus Christ with his atonement power of the Holy Spirit and the light of Christ to be saved and to be shifted into Christ consciousness of oneness with God.

Christ consciousness is when the heart and the mind of your soul are filled with the fullness of the Holy Spirit and the light of Christ with multicolor light shining like rainbow within your soul. This is the purpose Jesus Christ was sent to earth by our God-Parent to teach us how to do it through his apostles. In short, you must combine your prayer with meditation and fasting to connect directly with Jesus Christ, to receive the fullness of the Holy Spirit and the light of Christ, to activate your shift from human consciousness of separation from God to Christ consciousness of oneness with God.

Jesus said, "Nobody cometh to the Father but by me" (John 14:6). He said again, "It is the Father's desire that you receive His kingdom in all its fullness" (Luke 12:32). The choice yours.

The Great Mission of Jesus Christ on Earth

Jesus Christ came to earth with a divine plan from God that contained the blueprint on how to save the entire human race and the planet. The purpose of his divine mission was to bring the entire human race out from the spiritual darkness of sin and death, which they inherited from Adam and Eve, into the spiritual Light of Christ, through his atonement power of the Holy Spirit and the light of Christ, which is also called the grace or the body and the blood of Christ, which we must eat and drink symbolically.

According to the divine plan, Jesus Christ is saying today that we are now in the Christ-awakening age—the age where the entire human race must learn how to open up the heart of their souls through prayer meditation and fasting to connect directly with Jesus Christ himself to receive the atonement power of the Holy Spirit and the Light of Christ in the heart of their souls.

The receiving of the Holy Spirit and the Light of Christ in the heart of their souls will then raise their spiritual-energy vibration to create a shift from their human consciousness life of separation from God to Christ consciousness life of oneness with God, which will enable them to prophecy, to see visions and dream dreams. This then fulfils the prophecy by God that says, "And it shall come to pass in the last days, I will pour out my spirit upon all flesh, and your sons and your daughters shall prophecy, your young men shall see visions, and your old men shall dream dreams" (Acts 2:17).

There is also another prophesy by Jesus Christ himself that says, "Behold I stand at the door and knock if any one hear my voice and open the door, I will come in to him, and sup with him and he with me" (Revelation 3:20). This means opening up your heart of your soul with prayer, meditation, and fasting for Jesus Christ to come into the heart of your soul to awaken your personal Holy Spirit and for the light of Christ to shine within the heart of your soul like rainbow and to remove all the spiritual darkness of sin and death from your soul, which you have inherited from Adam and Eve, so that you might not die. Jesus said again, "He that believeth in me shall never die." "I come that you might have life, and that you might have it more abundantly." John 10:10b.

When Jesus Christ comes to awaken the Holy Spirit and the light of Christ in the heart of your soul, during your prayer, meditation, and fasting, you will experience a feeling of immense joy and peace, and you will see the light of Christ as multicolored light or rainbow within yourself with the inner eyes of your soul.

"And this will be your personal testimony, that the kingdom of God is within you, as the Light of Christ. For God is Light, and in Him there is no darkness at all" (1 John 1:5). As a Christian, you must always meditate to go deep within the heart of your soul temple and meet with Jesus Christ to receive divine directions for your life. This means to "trust the Lord with all your heart and lean not to your own understanding, in all your way acknowledge Him and He will direct your path" (Proverbs 3:5–6). Why? It's because you are a temple of God, and the temple is the meeting place of God and man. The heart of your soul is the holy of holies of your soul temple, where you meet with God and Jesus for all your prophecies and visions. Paul said. "Know ye not that your body is the temple of God and that the spirit of God dwells in you" (1 Corinthians 3:16).

You combine your prayer with meditation and fasting to go into the heart of your soul temple to meet with the spirit of God and Jesus Christ. This was the spiritual communication process by which all the apostles were able to receive all their revelations and wrote them down as the Bible that we are reading today. Jesus Christ taught them how to communicate.

Jesus said, "I Am the way, the truth and the life. Nobody come to the Father but by Me" (John 14:6) and "For God so love the world, that He gave His only begotten son that whosoever believed in Him shall never die but have everlasting life" (John 3:16). This means that our God-Parent has given our beloved Jesus Christ all the powers of heaven and earth, including the divine plan to come and redeem us all from the bondage of Satan's spiritual darkness of sin and death, which we inherited from Adam and Eve.

The Divine Plan Introduced by Jesus Christ on Earth

Jesus Christ began to introduced the divine plan when Nicodemus, a Pharisee and a leader of the Jews, came to Jesus by night and said to him, "Rabbi, we know that you are a teacher came from God: for no man can do these miracles except God be with Him" (John 3:1–2).

Jesus answered him, "Verily verily I say unto you, except a man be born again, he cannot see the kingdom of God" (John 3:3).

Nicodemus then said to Jesus, "How can a man be born when he is old? Can he enter the second time into his mother's womb and be born?" (John 3:4)

Jesus answered again, "Verily verily I say unto you, except a man be born of water and of the Holy Spirit, he cannot enter into the kingdom of God. That which is born of the flesh is flesh; and that which is born of the spirit is spirit. Marvel not that I say to you that, you must be born again" (John 3:5–7).

Jesus Christ is talking about two forms of birth. First is the birth of the flesh, which is human birth by human parent, with human body, human blood, and human consciousness. The second birth is of the spirit, which is Christ birth by the power of the Holy Spirit and the light of Christ from God. That means you are to be born again spiritually, as Christlike being with Christ body, Christ blood, and Christ consciousness to enable you to enter the kingdom of God because flesh and blood cannot enter the kingdom of God.

The most important point that Jesus Christ want all the Christians to understand is that all life begins at conception first before birth, whether physical life or spiritual life. But conception too will not come unless Alpha and Omega come together to make divine love, for Alpha to plant the seed of Christ child in the womb of Omega.

Then where is Alpha and where is Omega?

God the Father, God the Son, and God the Holy Spirit are all in the Alpha position, while your physical body, your soul, and your spirit are all in the Omega position. The coming together of Alpha and Omega to make divine love for Alpha to plant the seed of Christ child in the womb of Omega is called the baptism of the Holy Spirit and the light of Christ. Therefore, the baptism of the Holy Spirit and the light of Christ is Christ conception.

This does not mean that you are born again right away. It is just the beginning. It is like turning on your car engine. When the car engine is turned on, that doesn't mean that the car has reached its destination, but the engine has to be fed with fuel for the car to be able to travel to its destination. The same is true with Christ conception. This time, the Christ conception takes place in the heart of your soul. Once the seed of Christ child is conceived in the heart of your soul, the next thing to do is to feed it to grow and reach its maturity to be born.

The seed of Christ child has so many names in the Bible. It is called "the hidden man of the heart" (1 Peter 3:4), the divine manchild, "Christ in you the hope of glory" (Colossians 1:27), "Greater is He who is in you, than is he who is the world" (1 John 4:4), and "I can do all things in Christ who strengthens me" (Philippians 4:13).

The seed of Christ child is perfect already and has all the image and likeness of God and all the characteristics of Jesus Christ. It has Christ body, Christ blood, and Christ consciousness, including God body, God blood, and God consciousness, but it's just a tiny little baby that has to be fed to grow to reach its maturity to be born.

Then how do you feed it to grow? And with what type of food?

Jesus Christ came up with the answer and said,

I AM that bread of Life. Your fathers did eat manna in the wilderness, and are dead. This is the bread which came down from heaven, that a man may eat thereof, and not die. I AM the living bread which came down from heaven: if any man eat of this bread, he shall live forever: and the bread that I will give is my fresh, which I will give for the life of the world. (John 6:48–51)

The Jews therefore strove among themselves, saying, how can this man give us his flesh to eat? Then Jesus Christ said unto them, Verily verily I say unto you. Except you eat the flesh of the son of man, and drink His blood you have no life in you. Whoever eat my flesh, and drink my blood had eternal life; and I will raise him up at the last day. For my flesh is meat indeed, and my blood is drink indeed. He that eat my flesh, and drink my blood, dwells in me, and I in him. As the living Father had sent me, and I live by the father: so he that eat me, even he shall live by me. This is the bread which came down from heaven: not as your fathers did eat manna, and are dead: he that eat of this bread shall live forever. (John 6:53–58)

I will repeat the question: how do you feed the seed of Christ Child that is conceived in the heart of your soul to grow? And with what type of food?

Jesus Christ comes to provide his body and the blood for you to eat and drink to feed the seed of Christ child in the womb of the heart of your soul to grow and to reach its maturity to be born. The body and the blood are spiritual. The blood is the Holy Spirit— energy-like electricity, and electricity produces light. The light is the spiritual body. The body is the light body that the Holy Spirit energy produced and is called Christ, the creative light being. Jesus Christ is the embodiment of this creative light being called Christ.

Jesus is the physical human body, and the inside of his physical human body is the Christ light body, godlike body, or the Son of God. In short, the Christ light body reside inside the physical body of Jesus. "And the word was made flesh and dwelt among us" (John 1:14).

What Jesus Christ is talking about is spiritual flesh and spiritual blood, which we must eat and drink spiritually; that is, we must use prayer, meditation, and fasting combined to connect directly with him spiritually and draw the atonement power of the Holy Spirit and the light of Christ, which is also called grace, into the heart of our souls to feed the seed of Christ child that has been conceived in our hearts to grow and expand until it reach its maturity to be born.

I will repeat, the Holy Spirit and the light of Christ, which is also called grace, serves as the spiritual food for the Christ child to eat and drink to grow.

Jesus Christ was using a symbolic language to describe his mission on earth from God the Father to the Jews in his time. There was such an enormous spiritual darkness on the planet, and the consciousness of the people at that time was very low, vicious, wicked, and unenlightened. Therefore, Jesus Christ took the necessary measures of hiding the truth in a symbolic language so that the truth might not fall into the hands of the wicked to use the truth for evil and destruction but rather fall into the hands of the righteous to use it for good works on earth and the glory of God.

Jesus said to his apostles, "To you is given to know the mysteries of the kingdom of God, but to the world, they are to be taught in parables." (Matthew 13:11) This means the truth must always be given to the righteous after they have heard, believed, and accepted the gospel of Jesus Christ and have expressed their faith in Christ and repented of their sins to receive forgiveness.

The Two Most Important Key Points or Statements that Jesus Christ Made to Nicodemus

Jesus said, "That which is born of the flesh is flesh; and that which is born of the spirit is spirit. Marvel not that I say to you that you must be born again" (John 3:6–7). This statement is the core, or the key phrase, of the whole message of Jesus Christ. It is the goal of what Jesus Christ wants to accomplish for earth and humanity, and all his mission is built around this core message. So all believers of Jesus Christ must focus their attention on this core message and apply it to transform themselves or to be born again spiritually.

In his core message, Jesus Christ did mention two types of birth, born of the flesh and born of the spirit (John 3:7–8). But nothing can be born unless that thing that is to be born is first conceived. Conception comes first before birth; all life begins at conception, either physical conception and a spiritual conception. All conceptions are based upon the principles of God's divine plan of Alpha and Omega in balanced action. This means the man focuses on alpha and the woman focuses on omega.

The coming together of the man alpha and the woman omega to make sacred love to conceive a child and to give birth to a human being with a physical flesh. "That which is born of flesh is flesh," said the Lord.

The next is the spiritual birth, which is also the same principles of God's divine plan of Alpha and Omega coming together to make divine love for Alpha to plant the seed of Christ child in the womb of Omega.

John the Baptist said, "I baptize with water for repentance, but He who is coming after me, is mightier than I, whose sandals I am not worthy to carry. He will baptize you with the Holy Spirit and with Fire" ((Matthew 3:11). The Fire is white fire, the light of Christ that the Holy Spirit produces, like the cloven tongues on the heads of the apostles on the day of Pentecost, but this time it will be in the heart of your soul. This time, the Christ conception takes place in the heart of your soul. The next thing to do is to feed the seed of Christ child that is conceived in the womb of the heart of your soul to grow and reach maturity to be born.

Every word or statement that Jesus made had two meanings: surface meaning and spiritual meaning. Jesus is talking about spiritual body (or spiritual bread) and also spiritual blood (or spiritual wine) that you must eat and drink to feed the seed of Christ child that is conceived in the womb of the heart of your soul to grow. The spiritual blood is the Holy Spirit energy. The spiritual body is the Christ light body that the Holy Spirit produces.

How do you eat and drink the spiritual body and the spiritual blood that Jesus Christ has given you? You receive it by combining your prayer with meditation and fasting to connect directly with Jesus Christ Himself spiritually.

What does prayer do? What does meditation do? And what does fasting do?

Prayer is talking to God and asking God for your desires in the form of spiritual energy communication or transmission to Jesus Christ. "Jesus said, nobody cometh to the Father but by me." (John 14:6)

Meditation is listening to God and Jesus Christ intuitively; that is, being in tune with Jesus Christ to receive the energy of the Holy Spirit and the light of Christ in the heart of your soul as the spiritual food to feed the seed of Christ child that is conceived in the heart of your soul to grow. This spiritual food is also called Grace. Salvation is by grace.

Fasting removes all the spiritual energy blocks and the restraining forces from your body and your soul. This allows the Holy Spirit energy to flow freely through your body and your soul into your heart to feed the seed of Christ Child to grow and expand throughout your whole body, soul, and spirit This was the reason why Jesus Christ had to fast for forty days and forty nights to empower himself for his mission as an example to teach us, even though he was pure and holy in every respect. His apostles did the same thing.

Jesus Christ taught his apostles how to combine their prayer with meditation and fasting to connect directly with him to receive their final empowerment of the Holy Spirit and light of Christ on the day of Pentecost.

Jesus commanded his apostles and said to them, go throughout the whole world, and teach all nations and baptized them with the Holy Spirit. He said in Mathew 28:19, "Go ye therefore and teach all nations baptizing them in the name of the Father the Son and the Holy Spirit, teaching them to observe all things whatsoever I have commanded you, for I am with you all way even unto the end of the world."

The Holy Christ Command from Jesus to the Apostles

The apostles were the first people to receive the Christconsciousness empowerment, which means they have received the fullness of the Holy Spirit and light of Christ—their Christ body, Christ blood, and their Christ consciousness has been fully formed in them.

They are to go throughout the whole world to impregnate every heart of every soul on earth with the seed of Christ child through the baptism of the Holy Spirit and the light of Christ. Why? Because every soul on earth has to be born again spiritually, and that which is to be born has to be conceived first.

All life begins at conception or conception comes first before birth. But conception too will not come unless Alpha and Omega comes together to make divine love for Alpha to plant the seed of Christ child in the womb of Omega.

Then where is Alpha and where is Omega?

God the Father, God the Son, God the Holy Spirit, including all the apostles, are all in the Alpha position. Whiles you, your physical body, your soul, and your spirit are all in the Omega position. This means the whole human race is in the Omega position to receive Christ-child impregnation from the apostles of Jesus Christ through the baptism of the Holy Spirit. The coming together of Alpha and Omega to make divine love for Alpha to plant the seed of Christ child in the womb of Omega is called the baptism of the Holy Spirit and light of Christ. Therefore, the baptism of the Holy Spirit and the light of Christ is Christ conception. This is the beginning of Christconsciousness awakening in the heart of every soul on earth by Jesus Christ.

This time, the Christ conception, also known as the baptism of the Holy Spirit, has taken place in the heart of your soul, including every soul on earth by the apostles. The next thing to do is to feed the seed of Christ Child in the womb of the heart of your soul to grow and expand to reach its maturity to be born. How do you feed it, and with what food? You feed it by combining your prayer with meditation and fasting as your spiritual charger to connect directly with Jesus Christ himself to draw the Holy Spirit and the light of Christ energy into the heart of your soul to feed the seed of Christ Child to grow, just like how you would charge your cell phone with electricity. The Holy Spirit energy is the real blood of Christ. The light of Christ energy is the real body of Christ.

The seed of Christ child in the womb of your heart is already perfect and has all the image and likeness of God and all the characteristics of Jesus Christ. He has the Christ body, Christ blood, and Christ consciousness. But he is just a tiny little baby in the womb of the heart of your soul and needs to be fed to grow and reach its maturity to be born to replace your human body with Christ body, to replace your human blood with Christ blood and your human consciousness with Christ consciousness to enable you to enter the kingdom of God. Because flesh and blood cannot enter the kingdom of God, said the Lord Jesus Christ Why? Because the purpose of your flesh-and-blood body is to serve as a womb as well as your earthlife garment, and your earth-life Christhood-training uniform in the school where you learn how to become Christlike being and Jesus Christ is your teacher.

After you have fully developed your Christ garment, which is your Christ body, Christ blood, and Christ consciousness, then the next step is for it to come out—to be born. The old garment, which is your human body, human blood, and human consciousness that serves as a womb, begins to break apart for your Christ self to come out. Your human body returns to the dust. You don't need it anymore; it has served its purpose. From dust it came, to dust it must return.

You have now graduated from your earth-life Christhood training school with your new graduation garment and new credentials—Christ body, Christ blood, and the Christ consciousness—to receive a welcome home by Jesus Christ before our God-Parent. From God it came, to God it must return. "It is sown a natural body; it is raised a spiritual body. There is natural body, and there is a spiritual body" (1 Corinthians 15:44). The natural body consists human body, human blood, and human consciousness that served as a womb in which the seed of Christ child was conceived in the heart of the soul, through the baptism of the Holy and the light of Christ. "As we have borne the image of the earthy, we shall also bear the image of the heavenly" (1 Corinthians 15:49).

This is our journey from crucifixion to resurrection, then to ascension.

Crucifixion means to crucify all your sins of greed, lust, anger, hatred, revenge, stealing, covetousness and many more. All these create more spiritual darkness in your soul to disconnect you from God and Jesus Christ. Adam and Eve's sin of disobeying God commandment not to eat the forbidden fruit, caused by Satan's temptation, led to their fall into spiritual darkness of sin and death.

This is the position of the human race today. There is a veil of spiritual darkness of sin and death within our souls that we inherited from and Adam and Eve. This veil has to be removed from our souls by Jesus Christ to set us free from the chains or spiritual grip of Satan. This was the reason why Jesus Christ came to earth—to fight to tear down this veil of spiritual darkness of sin and death, with his atonement power of the Holy Spirit and the Light of Christ in the temple, as well as our own soul temples.

When Jesus Christ was crucified and was about to die on the cross, he declared "It is finished after he had drank a sponge filled with vinegar and gave up his spirit, and there came a great lightning from heaven that tore apart the veil inside the Jewish temple. The baptism of the Holy Spirit and the light of Christ is supposed to do the same thing in the heart of our soul temple.

Paul said in 1 Corinthians 3:16, "Know ye not that your body is the temple of God and that the spirit of God dwells you." The baptism of the Holy Spirit awakens the Christ light in the secret chamber of the heart of your soul. The Christ light, in turn, begins to push the spiritual darkness of sin and death out from your soul temple, and the veil of spiritual darkness of sin and death of Satan within your soul begins to fall apart. This is your enemy, the serpent head that must be crushed with the heel of your foot by Jesus Christ with his atonement power of the Holy Spirit to defeat Satan and save you as the seed of the woman, who are the children of Adam and Eve and also the children of the most high God.

God said to Satan and Adam and Eve in the garden of Eden in Genesis 3:15, "I will put enmity between thee and the woman, and between thy seed and her seed; it shall bruise thy head, and thou shall bruise his heel." This prophesy from God the Father to Adam and Eve in the garden of Eden predicts the victory of the seed of the woman—Christ, who would ultimately come to fight to give the church and mankind the power of the Holy Spirit and the light of Christ to defeat Satan, or to crush the serpent head, to save mankind and the church. This is where we are now.

The victory of the church and mankind are all set *as prophesied by God*. But what must the church and mankind do to make it happen? The answer is we all must focus our attention on Jesus Christ and listen to what he commands us to do and do it now.

How do we focus our attention on Jesus Christ to listen and to hear what he command us to do? You focus your attention by combining your prayer with meditation and fasting to connect directly with Jesus Christ himself spiritually to receive the atonement power of the Holy Spirit and the light of Christ in the heart of your soul first to feed the seed of Christ child in the womb of the heart of your soul to grow.

Second, you continue to draw the Holy Spirit and the light of Christ through prayer, meditation, and fasting to purify and to purge your soul to remove all the debris and contamination of spiritual darkness of sin and death from your soul, which you inherited from Adam and Eve. A typical example is how you use your cell phone charger to charge your cell phone with invisible electrical energy. You combine prayer, meditation, and fasting to serve as your spiritual charger to connect directly with Jesus Christ to receive or to draw the power of the Holy Spirit and the light of Christ into the heart of your soul.

Jesus said, "Unless you drink my blood and eat my flesh ye have no part with me" (John 6:53). He is referring to spiritual blood and spiritual body that you must drink and eat. The Holy Spirit energy is the blood. The light of Christ that the Holy Spirit produces is the body, the Christ-light body—your new garment.

Forgiveness of Sin

Our redemption begins with the forgiveness of sin by God. Forgiveness of sin is one of the greatest gifts that God has given to the human race to save themselves from destruction.

Forgiveness allow us to face the enemy within ourselves, which is the veil of spiritual darkness of sin and death that we inherited from Adam and Eve. Jesus Christ came to earth to redeem us from sin and death with his sacrificial blood and body on the cross. The blood represents the Holy Spirit energy, and the body represent the spiritual light body of Christ.

When a person repents of his or her sins and confesses his or her faith in Jesus Christ, that person receives forgiveness of all sins; God is not going to punish that person. But the contamination the sin created in your soul is still there, and if it is not cleansed, it will act out as a negative event in your life. Therefore, the next thing to perform is the baptism of the Holy Spirit and the light of Christ for the purification of your soul and also for your Christ-consciousness awakening by Jesus Christ. When a person has completed the awakening of his or her Christ consciousness by Jesus Christ, that person is now ready for the rapture.

The First Coming of Christ

The great mission of Jesus Christ on earth is divided into two parts. The first part is the first coming of Christ. The second part refers to the second coming of Christ.

The first coming of Christ is when Jesus Christ was conceived and born on earth by the power of the Holy Spirit by a virgin known as Mother Mary. Jesus Christ's first mission was to come to earth to plant the seed of Christ in the heart of every soul, including the heart of the planet Earth. This period is also called Christ conception age or time, the planting of the seed of Christ child in the womb of every heart of every soul on earth by Jesus Christ through the baptism of the Holy Spirit and the light of Christ. Because every soul has to be born again spiritually, including the planet.

The Christ seed in the womb of the heart of every person has to be fed with the sacred fire breath of the Holy Spirit to grow to reach its maturity and be born by Jesus Christ. How do you feed the Christ seed to grow? You combine your prayer with meditation and fasting to connect directly with Jesus Christ to receive the atonement power of the Holy Spirit and the light of Christ as the sacred fire breath to feed the Christ seed to grow.

The second coming of Christ is the Christ harvesting time, and the farmer is Jesus Christ, who comes to his farm to harvest his fruits. The fruits are the souls who have become sons and daughters of God or Christlike beings with Christ body, Christ blood and Christ consciousness to enable them to inherit the kingdom of God with Jesus Christ.

Paul said, "Therefore if any man be in Christ he is a new creature: old things are passed away; behold all things are become new" (2 Corinthians 5:17). That means, your old human body is changed into Christ body, your old human blood is changed into Christ blood, and finally your old human consciousness is also changed into Christ consciousness. When every person on earth has completed his or her awakening into Christ consciousness, he or she will be able see and hear Jesus Christ and talk to him. This is the goal of Jesus Christ, including our heavenly Father/Mother God.

Our God-Parent wants all of us to return home with our new garment, the Christ body with Christ consciousness, also known as the crystalline solar light body similar to Jesus Christ, capable of teleporting itself into any part of the holy light universe.

This is our divine birthright whether we believe it or not. We didn't create ourselves. God created us and planted the seed of Christ powers in us; therefore, he knows us more than we know ourselves. All we have to do is to surrender to his holy will and align ourselves with his divine plan, and we all shall be like Jesus Christ—because he is the blueprint as to how we all should become according to the divine plan of our God parent.

"What is man that thou art mindful of him he has created him a little lower than the angel and has crowned him with glory and honor" (Psalm 8:4–6).

The Establishment of the Church of Jesus Christ on Earth

The church of Jesus Christ was built upon the foundation of apostles, prophets, pastors, teachers, and evangelists with the chief corner stone being Jesus Christ himself. The twelve apostles were the first disciples or students to be taught by Jesus Christ about the kingdom of God and how to enter. Jesus Christ gave the apostles the master blueprint of the divine plan and taught them how to teach the world.

The apostles were the first group of disciples to complete the awakening of their Christ consciousness as taught by Jesus Christ on earth. Their assignment was to go throughout the whole world and plant the seed of Christ child in the womb of every heart of every soul on earth through the baptism of the Holy Spirit and the light of Christ.

Jesus Christ commanded his apostles,

> Go ye therefore and teach all nations baptizing them in the name of the Father, the Son and of the Holy Spirit, teaching them to observe all things whatsoever I have commanded you, for I am with you always even unto the end of the world. (Matthew 28:19)

That means God the Father, God the Mother, God the Son, and God the Holy Spirit, who form the supreme family of the universe are here to reclaim their children and planet earth back into their celestial home or the glory of God through the apostles. This fulfils the admonition of Jesus Christ, "Thine kingdom come thine will be done on earth as it is heaven" (Matthew 6:9). And again, we reflect, "What is man that thou art mindful of him He has created him a little lower than the angels and has crown him with glory and honor" (Psalm 8:4–6).

Royal children of the most high God, it's time to return home. All you have to do is to combine your prayer with meditation and fasting to connect directly with Jesus Christ spiritually to receive the baptism, which is the atonement power of the Holy Spirit and the Light of Christ, to feed the seed of Christ child in the womb of the heart of your soul to grow, and expand to push the spiritual darkness of sin and death from your soul, which you inherited from Adam and Eve. You must continue to expand as multicolored light, like rainbow within your soul until there is no more darkness left in your soul, and you will see it as your testimony with the inner eyes of your soul.

This Christ Light constitute the awakening of your Christ consciousness. Christ-consciousness person is a being of pure divine love, master of love, wisdom, power, illumination, compassion, kindness, peace, understanding, and mercy, just like Jesus Christ.

This is our divine destiny, and our God-Parent are in control. They want us to return home as Christlike beings, with our Christ body, Christ blood, and Christ consciousness, as our heavenly wedding garment of the Lamb of God for all eternity.

The Second Coming of Christ

The purpose of this book is very simple; that is, I am not going to get into all the stories of the adamic age, Abrahamic age, and the age of Moses and Pharaoh and so on but rather show to my readers the points that will help them envision the total picture of the spiritual journey of the human race from the earth to heaven, and from the human consciousness of separation from God to Christ consciousness of oneness with God.

The most important point is the knowledge of good and evil that was planted in the soul of Adam and Eve after they disobeyed God by eating the forbidden fruit of knowledge of good and evil caused by Satan's temptation (Genesis 3:6). The "knowledge of good" focuses on the Holy Spirit, the Light of Christ, heaven, Jesus Christ, God, immortality, and eternal life. The "knowledge of evil" focuses on the spiritual darkness of Satan, Lucifer, hell, sin, and death.

These two forces live side by side within the soul of every man and woman on earth today because all of the human race are descendants of Adam and Eve. The point where these two forces meet in the soul is called the duality consciousness—the human consciousness, the battleground, the separation from God consciousness. You are to use your free will to choose which side you want. If you choose good and righteousness, the Holy Spirit and the spiritual light of Christ, and love, this will then connect your soul back to Jesus Christ and the presence of God and eternal life. But if you chose evil, hatred, and sin, the spiritual darkness of Satan will lead your soul to death and hell. The choice is yours to determine your destiny. In the garden of Eden, God said to Adam and Eve, "Of every tree in the garden you can freely eat, but the tree of knowledge of good and evil, you shall not eat it. And the day that you eat it, you shall surely die, nevertheless you have your free will." (Genesis 2:16–17)

Another most important key point is the gift of free will to choose. Earth life is a spiritual journey to heaven or hell. Heaven is a high-energy world, while hell is a low-energy world. Good and evil have now been established in the soul of every man and woman by God and Satan. It is up to the human race to use their gift of free will to choose to go to heaven or to hell.

Earth life is a spiritual battleground where good and evil meet to battle over the soul, and it is also a Christhood training school set up by God, with Jesus Christ is our teacher to teach us what is good and what is evil to make our choices.

Good raises our spiritual energy and vibration of love, gives us peace, harmony, happiness, and all the good things in life, and finally awakens the light of our Christ consciousness to see and hear God. Sin or evil lowers our spiritual-energy vibration to create darkness of antichrist, to gives us pains, suffering and death in life, and to finally wind up in the low-energy vibration world, or spiritual prison.

The choices we make determine our destiny, whether to go to heaven or spiritual prison. God doesn't chose for us; we chose for ourselves—we are the authority for our destiny. "Chose ye this day whom ye will serve" (Joshua 24:14–15). God is not in the business of creating hell and sending people to hell or spiritual prison. He is in the business of creating heaven and sending people to heaven. Satan is the one who is in the business of creating hell and sending people to hell, and it is up to us to choose where we want to go.

If you chose good, then you must confess your faith in Christ, renounce all your sins, and chose the path of righteousness to generate light in your soul to transform your soul into a Christlike being with Christ consciousness to enable your soul to go to heaven or to enter into the kingdom of God, said the Lord Jesus Christ. And if you chose evil, then you must confess your faith in Satan and choose the path of sin to generate darkness in your soul to transform your soul into a demon and your spirit into an evil spirit and carry your soul to hell or spirit prison. With this understanding, you will be able to see through the whole Bible to envision what God's divine plan for humanity and the earth is and also the evil plan of Satan for the same.

The whole earth's spiritual project is a creative challenge between God and Satan, light and darkness, Christ and antichrist. In short, earth life is a Christhood training school, or divine love training school, to teach us all to become masters of love by Jesus Christ.

Jesus said, "This is my commandment that you love one another even as I have loved you" (John 15:12).

The Adamic Age

The Spiritual Journey of the Human Race from Earth to Heaven or Hell

The spiritual journey of the human race from earth to heaven began with the story of Adam and Eve in the garden of Eden and their relationship with God the Creator of heaven and earth.

Genesis 1:1 says, "In the beginning God created heaven and earth." The Bible tells us that God then proceeds to create light, day and night, the stars in the sky, and all kinds of fish to live in the ocean, animals to live on the land, birds in the air, and finally the man, Adam—all in six days, and he rested on the seventh day.

Adam was the first man created by God. "And the Lord God formed man of the dust of the ground, and breathed into his nostrils the breath of life; and man became a living soul" (Genesis 2:7). After the creation of Adam, God then put Adam in the garden of Eden and gave him total dominion over everything in it, including the fish of the sea, the birds of the air, and every living thing that moved on the earth.

After a certain period of time, God then saw that it was not good that Adam continued to remain alone. So God proceeded to create the first woman, Eve, by causing a deep sleep to fall on Adam and then took out one of his ribs. Then he commanded them to be fruitful and multiply and to fill the earth and subdue it.

> And the Lord God caused a deep sleep to fall on Adam, and he slept; and he took one of his ribs,

and closed up the flesh in its place. Then the rib which the Lord God had taken from the man. He made into a woman, and he brought her to the man. (Genesis 2:21).

After God had brought Eve to Adam to be his helper, Adam made a statement, "This is now bone of my bones and flesh of my flesh" (Genesis 2:22).

God also gave this mandate: "Therefore a man shall leave his father and mother and be joined to his wife, and they shall become one flesh" (Genesis 2:24).

Right from the beginning of creation of the first man and woman, God set up a holy union, marriage, based upon "bone of my bones and flesh of my flesh, and the two became one flesh," a spiritual union when the two marry with true love. The spiritual love bond holds them together for good.

Now the *stage is set*—God has now given the first man and first woman everything they need to be happy. He gave them total dominion over everything on earth. They also have their free will to choose and to be fruitful and multiply, which means they can produce children within the marriage union. Besides that, they have direct contact and fellowship with God. The Bible said God walked in the garden of Eden, where they were now living. However, there was one sure thing God forbade them not to eat—the tree of knowledge of good and evil.

> "The Lord God commanded the man, saying 'From any tree of the garden you may eat freely, but from the tree of knowledge of good and evil you shall not eat, for in the day that you eat from it you will surely die nevertheless you have your free will.'" (Genesis 2:16, 17)

The stage was set by God for Adam and Eve not to eat from the forbidden tree of knowledge of good and evil.

The Temptation of Satan

Satan appeared to Eve in the form of a serpent.

> Now the serpent was more cunning than any beast of the field which the Lord God had made. And he said to the woman, "Has God indeed said, you shall not eat of every tree of the garden?"

> And the woman said to the Serpent, we may eat the fruits of every tree in the garden; but of the fruit of the tree which is in the midst of the garden, God has said, "You shall not eat it, nor shall you touch it, lest you die."

> Then the Serpent [Satan] said to the woman, "You will not surely die. For God knows that, in the day you eat of it your eyes will be opened, and you will be like God, knowing good and evil."

This statement from Satan to the woman was, in fact, a direct challenge to God's word. The woman was convinced by Satan's deceptive persuasion. "So when the woman saw that the tree was good for food, and was pleasant to the eyes, and a tree desirable to make one wise, she took of its fruit and ate. She also gave to her husband to eat." (Genesis 3:6) Eve was the first person to sin by eating the forbidden fruit, followed by Adam when he took the fruit from Eve and ate.

"Then the eyes of both of them were opened, and they knew that they were naked." Their old sense of innocence was gone and was replaced with a new sense of knowledge of good of and evil. "And they sewed fig leaves together and made themselves coverings" for their nakedness. They saw themselves changed—a new consciousness had awaken in them.

There was a reduction of spiritual light of God and the awakening of spiritual darkness of Satan in their soul. This created a shift in their awareness to see both sides of good and evil, and as such, their fellowship with God was reduced. Their bodies were also changed from physical light bodies of immortality to physical dense bodies of mortality. The physical light body has 100 percent spiritual light of God in the soul, and as such, it cannot die and can only see God. Sin creates spiritual darkness in the soul, and spiritual darkness creates disconnection from God and death. This is the position of the human race today. This new consciousness or awareness is called the human consciousness. It is the point where good and evil meet, light and darkness meet to fight over the soul of man and woman. It is the battle ground for the human race at the physical and spiritual level to give them the opportunity to exercise their free will to choose right or wrong, God or Satan, light or darkness, Christ or antichrist. The stage is now set by God to produce the human race with human consciousness from the seed of Adam and Eve to populate the earth. God said to Adam and Eve, "Be fruitful and multiply" from now on.

All human race must experience the influence of good and evil, light and darkness, Christ and antichrist for you to use your free will to learn how to make right choices and practice it until it becomes part of you—master of love.

If you choose the light of Christ, good, and righteousness, then you must practice the life of good and righteousness and the light of Christ until your soul is completely filled with the light of Christ, love, good, and righteousness. There will be no more darkness or evil left in your soul. This means that the light of Christ has eliminated the spiritual darkness of evil or antichrist from your soul completely, and you are now one with God and Jesus Christ. This means that you have now shifted from your human consciousness of separation from God to Christ consciousness of oneness with God.

You have experienced the spiritual darkness of Satan before. You know all about it, and you don't need it anymore in your life. You are now free from it, you only want the Holy Spirit and the light of Christ in your soul, and that is all you need for your eternal life in heaven with Jesus Christ.

The spiritual doorway to heaven

Your spiritual doorway to heaven is in the secret chamber of the heart of your soul temple, and only you—and you alone—have the key to open and enter. There's no one else because you are the priest or priestess of your own soul temple.

Priesthood means the ability to use meditation to go inside the heart of your soul temple to communicate with the spirit of God. Apostle Paul said, "Know ye not that your body is the temple of God and that the spirit of God dwells in you" (1 Corinthians 3:16).

Meditation gives you direct access to your deeper self. It allows you to see inside of your soul to examine your own spiritual position in life in the presence of Jesus Christ. "Draw nigh to God and He will draw nigh to you," said by Jesus Christ (James 4:8). Focus your attention on Jesus and Jesus too will focus his attention on you, to give you your desires.

<u>*The Journey to Heaven*</u>

Meditation is what you used to invite him to come into your temple. Meditation is listening to God. Prayer is talking to God. Meditation is receiving energy from God and Jesus into your heart, mind, and soul. Prayer is transmitting energy from your heart, mind, body, and soul containing your desires to God and Jesus to be fulfilled.

Christ Awakening Meditation and Prayer Centers for All Churches

Why is this needed? Because as a Christian, you must use prayer and meditation to connect directly with Jesus Christ to receive the Christ light energy of the Holy Spirit to cleanse your soul from all your sins to save yourself from Satan and carry your soul to heaven.

The darkness of antichrist in our souls serves as Satan's power grip to keep us in his chains on earth to pull our souls down to hell, or his underworld of darkness. That which created the darkness of antichrist in our soul was the sin that we inherited from Adam and Eve.

The journey to heaven begins from the heart of your soul. It is the awakening of the divine spark of the holy Christ fire in the heart of your soul and your ability to go within the heart of your soul and connect with it and use it to invite Jesus Christ to come into your soul temple to purge and cleanse you from all your sins that have created the spiritual darkness in your soul. The light of Christ, or the divine spark of the Holy Spirit, will take over your soul and carry you to heaven. This is called Christ consciousness.

The tools to use to control and to connect with the Christ power in the heart of your soul is meditation and prayer combined with fasting. Your mastery of meditation, prayer, and fasting are the keys to complete your journey to heaven.

Jesus wants to meet with you personally within your temple of your soul. Your body and soul were created to be the temple of God. A temple is the meeting place of God and man to do business, and Jesus wants to meet with you in your Temple.

Confess your faith in Christ and renounce your sins and choose the path of love and righteousness to generate light in your soul to propel your soul to heaven.

The Divine Nature of Man and Woman

We were brought into life or existence by a divine family who owed their mysterious existence to themselves. They were the beginning of all things visible and invisible in the whole creation. These first mysterious beings known as Alpha and Omega gave birth to us as light beings and called us *souls*. Our first habitation place was in their presence as infant souls to be nurtured by our God parent in the glory of God.

The main focus of the soul development was the heart and mind, specifically the intuitive power of the heart and intellectual power of the mind. These are the two main power centers of the divine nature of man and woman. The goal in life is to develop these two power centers in your soul and use them to run your lives and be in partnership with Jesus Christ to assist God to run and expand his creation in harmony and in peace. How do you develop them? It is through constant prayer, meditation, and fasting to connect directly with Jesus Christ to receive the Holy Spirit and the light of Christ in the heart of your soul on earth now to prepare you for the rapture to begin.

It's an exciting time for humanity and the church world. "'In the last days I will pour out my spirit upon all flesh,' said the Lord God."

Man, Know Thyself

What is the nature of man as created by God with his many levels of consciousness?

First, man has a (1) physical body, (2) soul body, (3) spiritual body, or the Christ body, and the (4) i am that i am body. The last body can also be called the God body because they are the image of God in man.

The physical body is a garment or uniform with separate consciousness that is wrapped around the soul. The consciousness is what we might refer to as human consciousness or lower consciousness. Your consciousness is your awareness, becoming aware of yourself as a separate being with a sense of self.

There are five senses in the human consciousness: sight, hearing, smell, taste, and touch. These five senses give the human body the awareness to function at its level of life in the human world. The senses make him a separate being with a mind capable of functioning with his own power of consciousness, and the consciousness is divided into conscious mind and the subconscious mind. The *conscious* mind is the messenger who is always ready to act now to fulfill your request. The *subconscious* mind is the messenger who stores your information in the memory bank for future use. It stores both good and evil information to be retrieved and used by the conscious mind when the need arises for the human consciousness to act.

The human consciousness can rise above its level and connect with the soul consciousness by opening up its sixth and seventh senses through meditation on Jesus Christ. Sixth and seventh senses are all made up of light sensors, which is like turning on the light bulbs from a specific wiring system in the soul and physical body to connect them together, and this can be done by Jesus Christ through meditation. This interconnectivity of the soul can now be extensions to the light body of Christ within the soul with Christ consciousness Herein lies the power of man and woman. This is what we might call self-realization of the spirit of God in the soul of man and woman, God in man and woman who know their own divine self, or Christ in man and woman who know their own divine self. This is what Jesus Christ wants every Christian to reach. When you have reached this level, called Christ consciousness, you are now in partnership with God and Jesus Christ to run his creation. The kingdom of God is now yours by your divine birthright forever, and you will always take a stand to defend that which is yours against Satan, just like Jesus Christ.

This is the path that I personally have chosen, and I am asking you to choose the same path. Enlightenment is the never-ending truth that comes directly from the great central light being called God, to be expressed in the physical human world as well as the universe as divine plan from God.

Meditation

Meditation, meditation, meditation is the key.

Meditation allows us to gain access to the personal Christ within our soul. It also gives us access to Jesus Christ to invite him to come into our soul temple and request healing from him.

Meditation allows us to gain access to the planetary Christ light energy, solar Christ light energy, and the universal Christ light energy to draw to feed the Christ light in the heart of our soul to glow. Jesus Christ calls this energy as "fountain," "river of life," and a "wellspring" of everlasting life. Therefore, we have enough Christ light energy to change the condition of our soul, body and mind into Christ-like beings.

We can change the conditions on earth if we will learn how to draw the Christ light energy into our souls and radiate it out for healing through meditation. Jesus wants to come into our body temples, but we must meditate to invite him first.

Our Human Nature

The nature of who we are consists of two parts. The first part of ourselves is the supply part, and the second part is the need part.

The need part consists of our physical body, which is always in need and wants so many things, like the food, water, clothes, and shelter, as well as cars, airplanes, ships, telephones and cell phones to communicate, including computers, television, and etc. It also wants to build families, societies, cities, nations, and countries.

It is the Creator and the creative part of you that can, and has the ability to, supply you with all your needs in the form of creative concepts and ideas. The tools to use to get these creative ideas and concepts is to use meditation to link your lower mind of your human physical body with a higher mind of the creative parts of you, in your soul.

The creative supply part of you is the spirit of God and the Christ within your soul that you must depend on at all times for your needs. Jesus said, "Draw near to God and He will draw near to you" (James 4:8). That means you draw closer to Christ within your soul, and Christ within your soul will draw closer to you to give you everything you need in the form of creative ideas and concepts to apply to get what you want. You must do this through meditation to establish the spiritual link between your two natures.

This is what constitutes the priesthood—the ability to use meditation and prayer to go within your soul temple to communicate with God and Christ to receive your needs. Those who have specialized in prophecies have become spokesmen of disaster as well as blessings from God.

Connecting Point

The heart of your soul is the connecting point to heaven, God, and Jesus Christ. In order to see and communicate with heaven, God, and Jesus Christ, you must look through the heart of your soul with your attention focus on Christ within you. This process is called meditation.

In the secret chamber of your heart is the holy Christ fire to link you to heaven and Jesus. At this point in time, you have become a high priest of your own body and soul temple because you can now enter into your temple at will through meditation.

There are so many lessons that the disciple on the path of priesthood must go through in the temple training, and each temple is equipped with a specific lesson the disciple must learn, practice, and master before he moves on to the next temple.

The purpose of this temple training is to transform the disciple into a priest of Christ, with Christ powers in him to enable him to communicate with God and Jesus Christ to receive divine direction to guide humanity to bring the kingdom of God on earth, not just being saved as popular belief we have in the churches today. There is far more to it than that—the Christ power in us is more powerful than death. As the Bible says, "Greater is he who is in you, than is he who is the world" and "Christ in you the hope of glory." (1 John 4:4) Therefore we become conquerors of death and God's kingdom builders after the temple priesthood training school is over.

These are some of the hidden teachings of Jesus Christ unbeknown to many Christian churches.

The Journey through the Mysteries of the Priesthood of Christ

This journey is divided into four parts, four distinct temple training to train the human race to become Christlike beings with Christ consciousness to able to communicate with Jesus Christ, God, and all the company of heaven. It is the new priesthood covenant of Christ that belongs to every man and woman by divine birthright.

The first is the temple of faith of the divine Father. The second is the temple of water baptism of John the Baptist. The third is the temple of fire baptism of Christ by Jesus. The fourth is that all of the Holy Spirit, the creative temple of the divine Mother.

The first lesson in the first temple is faith, like Abraham's faith in God. God the father introduced himself to Abraham and testified the coming of his Son, Christ, and made covenant and passed it on to Isaac, Jacob the Israel, to confess their faith in Christ and in God to renounce all their sins and chose the path of righteousness.

The purpose of righteousness, or righteous life, is to generate light in their souls to transform them into sons and daughters of God, or children of the most high God, to create God's kingdom on earth. "Thine kingdom come thine will be done on earth as it is in heaven" (Matthew 6:10).

Satan is also on earth to create an opposing power to God's kingdom. Therefore, he is saying to humanity, "Confess your faith in antichrist and renounce the path of righteousness and choose the path of sin to generate darkness in your soul to create the kingdom of Satan or hell on earth. The choice is yours to make."

"Chose ye this day whom ye will serve" (Joshua 24:15).

The Holy Priesthood of Jesus Christ Unveiled

He or she who can feel the Christ light in his or her heart and can see the Christ light in his or her mind is a priest or priestesses of Christ. All sons and daughters of God who have the spirit of God living in their soul body temples and can communicate with God in their temples are all priest and priestesses of God and Christ.

This priesthood is after the new and everlasting covenant introduced by Jesus Christ to his twelve apostles at the Last Supper. It connected the old priesthood of Melchizedek to the new priesthood of the Son of God together.

The beginning and the end were now joined together to create balance of power, harmony, and the beginning of the end times, the age of the Holy Spirit, which is the home-age of the divine Mother, Omega priesthood power, join with the Alpha priesthood power of the divine Father, including the priesthood power of the Son of God. "For as many as received him, to them gave ye power to become the sons of God," (John 1:12–13) as well as daughters of God. That is, anybody who received Jesus, whether a man or a woman, was given the power, the power of the priesthood of Christ. For without this Christ light power in your soul, you cannot go to heaven.

"Christ in me the hope of glory." (Colossians 1:17) My hope to return to the glory of God depends upon the Christ light power in the heart of my soul. Therefore, all men and women must receive this Christ light priesthood power to be saved. You cannot withhold this priesthood power from a woman.

The Priesthood Power

The priesthood power is the main source of spiritual power to connect the human race to God through the soul. This is called Christ-consciousness awakening.

The soul is the connecting point, and the power is located in the heart of the soul and is controlled by the mind of the soul within the head.

You are a soul living in a physical body. The Christ light power is in your heart. This is the presence of God in you, and as such you are a temple of God. You become a priest of your own temple when you are able to communicate with God in your own temple through meditation and prayer.

To make it more precise, when you, the physical body personality, are able to link and communicate with its internal soul personality through meditation. As such, the most important thing you must do is to do nothing but to listen within through meditation and ask your soul with prayer what you should do, then follow your inner guidance. In this way, the guiding hands of God will direct your life into the self-mastery you seek.

I will call this the soul path. That means you must meditate every morning to listen to the soul voice within and follow its divine direction for everything you do, so to speak. This is what Jesus Christ wants the church to teach its members.

You must understand that as a priest of your own temple, you are responsible for the upkeep of the temple. The temple must be kept clean because every day that you meditate, the kingdom of God becomes tangible or visible within you, said the Lord Jesus. You and God are one now. You are not just an ordinary person anymore—you are God's ambassador on earth. You represent him for him to work through you. That makes you a priest of the most high God on earth.

This is the key to the building of the priesthood nation as well as the priesthood kingdom on earth. This is the ultimate goal of Jesus and God the creators of all things.

When God is living in all things, then there is harmony and peace because he created them, and all things belong to him. Yours is to learn to share with the divine parents and assist in their divine plan as children of the holy one who holds the Christ priesthood powers on earth.

The Family

You can make your own choices by your free will, and it has to be in alignment with God's plan of Alpha and Omega to save yourself from troubles.

Many people have chosen celibate life, and they have to make sure whether it is in alignment with the principles of Alpha and Omega.

Many people argue that a woman cannot hold the priesthood. They must make sure whether their argument is in accordance with the principles of Alpha and Omega, which resonates from the creative core and moved throughout the whole universe. Because if there is Alpha priesthood, then there should be Omega priesthood also.

Masculine priesthood, feminine priesthood, father priesthood, mother priesthood—the priesthood of God belongs to every gender, not to a handful of men. Why? Because God wants to build priesthood cities of God, priesthood nations with priesthood families to produce Christlike children with Christ body, Christ blood, and Christ consciousness to establish the kingdom of God on earth, or a priesthood planet.

If God the Father will bear the title father, and God the Mother will bear the title mother and will not produce any children, the whole universe will be empty and will not make sense, there will be no purpose for God to create, and God will have nothing to do.

If God will produce children, then there should be a habitation for his children to live and enjoy their lives the God-Parent has given them. This led to the creation of the universe.

The spiritual goal of Jesus Christ for earth and humanity is to create spiritual light of Christ in the heart of our souls and carry our souls to heaven. This is called Christ consciousness.

Meditation and prayer are some of the spiritual tools provided by Jesus Christ to his apostles.

Meditation allows you to go within your soul to contact the spirit of God and the light of Christ in the heart of your soul. Righteousness generates light in your soul. Prayer allows you to talk to the spirit of God and the light of Christ in the heart of your soul directly. From the heart of your soul, your prayer is then carried to heaven, to Jesus, and to God the Father to be fulfilled.

God put a portion of his spirit in Adam when he breath through Adam the breath of life and he became a living soul. We as offspring of Adam and Eve inherited the same characteristics as our birthright. When the spirit of God and light of Christ are fully awakened in us by Jesus Christ through meditation and prayers, it will transform us all into sons and daughters of God, into priests and priestesses of our own soul Temples. This is what Jesus wants the church to teach its members to transform the world from the darkness of Satan.

The battle is between the light of Christ and the darkness of Satan over the soul of men and women and the planet Earth. The soul must choose light and righteousness and reject sin and darkness of Satan.

Righteousness generates the light of Christ in the soul, and sin generates darkness of Satan in the soul. Use your free will to choose, which one you want and reject the other one. You are here on earthly schoolroom to experience both good and evil and to choose which one you want and graduate in it—as Christlike beings with Christ consciousness to enable you to live in heaven or as antichrist being to live in hell with Satan.

The spiritual goal of Satan is to create darkness in our souls, to carry our souls to hell through sin. The devil has worked so hard to make sure that humanity and the Christian world are not able to recognize the importance of meditation and prayers because they are the main keys to connect with God and Jesus Christ to receive power to defeat him. As soon as humanity and the Christian world are able to master the use of meditation and prayers to connect with their own internal powers of the spirit of God and the light of Christ in the heart of their souls, Satan will not stand a chance.

Here is where the holy army of Jesus Christ can be formed to provide a united front against the dark forces on the planet—cancel out all the negative prophecies that have been predicted in the Bible to take place on the planet. These negative prophecies are spiritual darkness that contain negative events to act out as prophecies. If they are not transmuted or cancelled out by the light of Christ, they will happen.

We must desire the spirit of God and the light of Christ with all our hearts and burning desire because that is the ultimate power that will give us our total victory over the devil as well as eternal life. Light brings blessings to mankind—blessings of peace, love, knowledge of prosperity and heaven. Darkness brings curse, pain, death, suffering, and hell to mankind. Choose which one you want.

I stand before you to challenge you all as a member of the holy army of Jesus Christ. This is our mission, and nobody can stop us.

Once your awareness has shifted into the light of Christ consciousness in your soul, you will never be the same again. Because you have now become aware of both the light and darkness within your soul. You must now continue to draw the light into your soul through meditation and prayer at all times to fight the darkness and increase your light until there is no more darkness left in your soul.

When the darkness of antichrist in our souls and in the planet are no more, then all those negative events as predicted prophecies will not happen because the dark energy that serves as the cause behind the negative event has been transmuted or cancelled out by the light of Christ, also known as the blood of Christ.

The light of Christ or the blood of Christ is the truth and grace that shall make you free, or make humanity free. This is the truth that we must pursue to free ourselves from Satan's grip. Once we come to know this knowledge and apply it, a change will surely come to earth and humanity will be free from Satan.

Your main goal is to gain direct access to the internal light of Christ in the heart of your soul. This is your personal Christ power, your Christ engine of eternal life, and it is your source of everything and your point of contact with Jesus Christ in heaven.

The Knowledge of Good and Evil

Right now in your life, good and evil meet within your soul to battle over your soul. You must use your free will to make your choice. You must choose good and reject evil to save your soul. This is what Jesus wants you to do now. This is what the church wants you to do now. The choice is yours.

Only you and you alone can use prayer and meditation to connect with the spirit of God and the light of Christ in the heart of your soul temple to communicate with Jesus Christ, and this is your point of contact.

Our earth life is a mortal schoolroom and a battleground. The fall of Adam and Eve created a mortal schoolroom of good and evil on earth, where souls could come from God to learn and experience good and evil and a proper use of free will and finally graduate with the spiritual attainment of Christ consciousness which will allow them to live in heaven with Jesus Christ.

The point where good and evil meets in the soul is called the human consciousness, the battleground. All human beings are in the world of good and evil, experiencing and learning with their human consciousness. Good and evil, light and darkness are always fighting with each other over the soul of man and woman to take control to lead them to good, Christ, and heaven, or to evil, Satan, and hell. We must use our free will to choose. If you chose good, then you must obey the laws of good actions from Jesus Christ, and you must also do what Jesus tells you to do for your salvation.

The Divine Plan of God

If Adam and Eve had not sinned, what would have been their position? If Adam and Eve had not sinned, they would have remained in the state of innocence, knowing no evil for they knew no sin.

You need to experience *sin* to appreciate good, pain and suffering to appreciate peace and happiness. We are in a school of knowledge of good and evil whether we understand it or not. You need to experience darkness to appreciate light. You need to experience evil to appreciate good, hatred to appreciate love, bad to appreciate good. At this stage, the divine plan of God, which is love, wisdom, and power, are brought into open view for all of us to see and experience, to perfect the human race into Christlike beings with Christ consciousness on earth, and finally to carry then to heaven by Jesus Christ. What took place in the garden of Eden between God and Satan, Adam and Eve, is what sets the stage of the destiny of the human race and the planet Earth. Adam and Eve became aware of good and evil when the fall occurred. Their state of innocence was changed. They have "become like one of us," that is, like God who knows good and evil.

The goal of life according to God's divine plan is to give the entire human race a spiritual training on what is good and what is bad or evil, what is light and what is darkness, and give them the gift of free will to choose good and reject evil, to choose light and reject darkness—to bring them into the glory of God as Christ light beings with Christ consciousness, not as human beings with human consciousness and body.

Things that Satan Do Not Want You to Know

My goal of this book is to set the stage by giving my readers the understanding of what God is trying to do, beginning from the garden of Eden.

This will open the door of the kingdom of God within the soul of everybody for them to see and enter with clarity and understanding of the knowledge of God. This will bring peace, harmony, and joy to earth. All of these negative prophecies that are predicted in the Bible can be transmuted or cancelled out with the light of Christ from God and Jesus Christ so that it will not happen. The energy of darkness, which was the driving cause, has been destroyed by the light of Christ, which is also known as the atonement power of Jesus Christ, or the blood of Christ, and humanity is free at last.

This is what Satan doesn't want us to know. You are in a school to study what is good and what is evil, and you have to use your free will to choose what you want and what to reject. This is God's divine plan to train you. Your understanding of this settles everything between you and God.

What the spiritual fall of Adam and Eve did was to establish the knowledge of good and evil, light and darkness, in the soul of Adam and Eve to start their mortal life experience. You are learning and experiencing how to use free will to make choices of good and evil and then finally appreciate good and the light of Christ. Having experienced good and evil, light and darkness in your mortal life, it is hoped that you will chose and appreciate good and light and reject evil and darkness.

Then comes the redeemer Jesus Christ with his atonement power of the Holy Spirit and the light of Christ to plant it in the heart of your soul to wipe out all your sins and darkness from your soul through prayer and meditation that you will use to draw him into your soul, into action. "Ask and ye shall receive, knock and it shall be open up unto you, seek and ye shall find." (Matthew 7:7)

You use prayer to connect and ask from Jesus what you want, and you use meditation to connect to receive it. You use prayer to ask for the power of the Holy Spirit from Jesus, and you use meditation to receive the power of the Holy Spirit from Jesus, into the *heart* of your soul for your rapture. It is a two-way communication system, not one way.

This understanding is what is missing in the Christian churches, which has to be restored to the average Christian to be empowered to fight to defeat Satan.

Christ-Consciousness Awakening Age

We are in the Christ-consciousness awakening age. All human beings must shift from their human consciousness life of separation from God, to the Christ consciousness life of oneness with God now.

Open your heart and your mind through prayer and meditation to connect directly with Jesus Christ to receive your Christ consciousness awakening to wipe out all your sins, to conquer death and Satan, and to be transformed to go through the rapture.

The Spiritual Daytime and Nighttime of the Soul

There are two spiritual events of the soul's journey to heaven or hell. They are spiritual nighttime of the soul and spiritual daytime of the soul.

The spiritual night of the soul began from the time of Adam and Eve. Adam and Eve were tempted by Satan to disobey God by eating the forbidden fruit. This caused their spiritual fall, and the light of God and Christ in their souls became dim or reduced and spiritual darkness took over their souls. The direct, open spiritual communication with God was completely reduced to the point of extinction, from spiritual light of God and Christ in their souls to the spiritual darkness of antichrist, called the dark night or spiritual fall of Adam and Eve.

Since we are the offspring of Adam and Eve, we have inherited this spiritual fall of darkness within our souls. Therefore, we are in the dark night of the soul. Romans 3:23 says, " For all have sinned and fall short of the glory of God." The spiritual darkness in our souls represents our personal antichrist and our personal nighttime. We must awaken, the light of Christ in the heart of our souls to shift from nighttime to daytime.

First, it started with the spiritual fall of Adam and Eve. The cause was the sin of Adam and Eve. The effect of sin invited a curse from God, which resulted in a loss of spiritual light of God in their souls to spiritual darkness. This loss of spiritual light of God disconnected them from the presence of God partially. Spiritual darkness entered into their souls. They became aware of light and darkness, good and evil, as well as right from wrong. Now they can see that they are naked. A new consciousness had awakened in them.

This new consciousness is called the human consciousness. The human consciousness is the battleground where light and darkness, good and evil, Christ and antichrist meet to fight over the soul.

Adam and Eve must now continue to use their free will to choose to do the right or wrong, light or darkness, obey God or Satan to direct their life on earth.

The history of the nighttime of the soul began from the Old Testament in the Bible, which chronicles the human soul's journey from spiritual darkness of Satan to spiritual light of Christ, God and heaven. The Old Testament is the old priesthood covenant between God and man, Abraham and his seed, Isaac, Jacob, and Joseph and the twelve tribes of Israel.

The New Testament is the new priesthood covenant between God and the entire human race, through the baptism of the Holy Spirit and the Christ light awakening in the heart of every soul on earth by Jesus Christ. The apostle Paul preached the Christ gospel to the gentile world, who receive Jesus Christ also.

The light of Christ awakened in every heart is the spiritual daytime of the soul, a new dawn of a golden age on earth. This period is the time of joy. The great spiritual war between light and darkness is over—Jesus Christ and the sons and daughters of God had won the battle. Earth has returned to its celestial home, the glory of God. This light of Christ will then propel you to heaven. This is your journey from crucifixion to resurrection then to ascension. Crucifixion means to crucify all of your sins and evil deeds because they do generate darkness in your soul to prevent you from going to heaven.

The final stage is ascension. Your soul and body are now filled with spirit of God and the light of Christ to carry you to heaven. The final battle and the spiritual journey from earth to heaven is now completed. The spiritual battle of good and evil, between God and Satan, over the soul of man and woman is over.

Personal Affirmation

1. I *am* a temple of God

2. The Spirit of God dwells inside my temple.

3. My ability to go inside my temple to communicate with the spirit of God to receive divine directions makes me a priest of my own temple.

4. This is what Jesus Christ wants everyone to become—a priest.

5. Christ and God are one; therefore, I carry Christ in my temple everywhere I go.

6. If I talk to Christ in my temple through meditation and prayers, he will respond to me by visions, dreams, and a small voice from the heart of my soul.

7. "Christ in you, the hope of glory."

8. "Greater is he who is in you, than is he who is in the world."

Your hope to return to the glory of God depend upon the awakening of the light of Christ consciousness in the heart of your soul by Jesus Christ.

Where is the kingdom of God and the throne?

The kingdom of God is within you, within your soul, and your heart is the throne of God. This means technically, you must bring your attention from your mind to connect with your heart and from your heart of your soul to link with Jesus Christ in heaven. This is called communion ("come in union") with Christ to receive spiritual light of Christ into your soul, and this must continue until your soul is full of light to vanquish the spiritual darkness in your soul.

You reach your Christ consciousness when you have been able to eliminate the darkness from your soul by the light of Christ completely. This is what is referred to as the atonement of Jesus Christ.

The Spiritual Doorway to Heaven

The spiritual doorway to heaven is in the secret chamber of the heart of your soul temple, and only you—and you alone—have the key to enter and no one else because you are the priest or priestess of your own temple.

Priesthood means the ability to use meditation to go inside of your soul temple to communicate with the spirit of God. Meditation gives you direct access to your deeper self. It allows you to see inside of your soul to examine your own spiritual position in life before Jesus Christ. "Draw nigh to me and I will draw nigh to you," said Jesus Christ. Focus your attention on Jesus, and Jesus too will focus his attention on you to give you your desires.

The Mission of Christ and Jesus to Humanity

The mission of Jesus was to come and awaken a planet that has fallen from a high-energy world to a low-energy world. Humanity and the planet fell as a unit; therefore, humanity and the planet must return to the high energy world as a unit.

What is a high-energy world? High-energy world is where God lives, the glory of God—heaven. High energy is pure energy. It is pure-energy world, also called holy light universe.

Energy has consciousness—pure consciousness, high consciousness, Christ consciousness, "i am that i am" consciousness, universal consciousness, and eternal consciousness. High-energy eternal life or high-energy body, is pure-energy body that has no flesh and blood and cannot die.

A high-energy being is a pure-energy being that has Christ consciousness and a high-energy body who lives in the presence of God. We sometimes call them holy spirits. You must have Christ consciousness and high energy body to be able to live in heaven, and Jesus is our example.

Here in this world of high energy, there is peace, creativity, harmony, love, compassion balance, beauty, and adventure into new frontiers of creative designs and learning. Here, you and God are one in creative harmony and peace for all eternity. This is real life.

You and your planet fell from this into the low energy world. The fall began with one rebellious child, whose name is Lucifer or Satan, and then infected the planet and humanity. Today, this planet is his base.

What is low-energy world? When energy falls from high to low, things become very difficult. When energy falls from high to low, it becomes impure energy, and impure energy is opposite to pure energy. Love is pure energy; hatred is impure energy. Therefore, hatred is opposite to love.

Satan or Lucifer was once a pure-energy being who fell from high energy to low energy from the love of God to the hatred of God; therefore, he cannot live in the presence of God or high-energy world.

You and your planet was once a pure-energy planet in a high-energy world in the presence of God, and all of you had Christ consciousness and divine love. Now you are here in the low-energy world, which is the fall. But you must return to the high-energy world. This is where Jesus comes in with the great master plan to jumpstart the holy Christ fire in the heart of humanity and the planet to accelerate their energy from low to high.

A low-energy world is a world at low consciousness, impure consciousness, antichrist consciousness, human consciousness, hatred, anger, sin, disease, and death—a world of hostilities and wars. It is a world where Lucifer or Satan use low-energy frequency waves to transmit his wicked intentions to those who are in tune to create wars, terrorism, and hostilities to destabilize the planet and humanity to keep them at low-energy level. Adolf Hitler, Osama Bin Laden, and Saddam Hussein are examples. The same is true with those who are in tune with high energy and bring love, peace, and creativity to the world. Examples are Jesus and his apostles and many others, like scientists. Look at what the science and technology has done to your world today.

The Voice of Jesus

Jesus insists that Christianity and humanity should stop having misguided understanding about "Jesus suffered for them and died to pay the price for their sins and that, his death on the cross had saved them." This is the truth that has been turned upside down to defeat the purpose why Jesus came from heaven to earth, from high-energy world to low-energy world of the Lucifer and his legions of darkness. It is carefully designed by the Luciferians on earth, to shift the Christians and humanity from their holy Christ consciousness, or the holy Christ fire within the secret chamber of their own hearts, to make sure it's completely shut down to keep them at low-energy level and powerless. Because when the Christ consciousness in the hearts of all the Christians and humanity is fully awakened, it will be like awakening the sleeping giants on the planet Earth. The Christed beings have finally awakened from their sleep to fight and crush the serpent's head, to defeat Satan without a single drop of blood.

The next thing that the Luciferians have done to humanity and Christianity is to focus their attention on the physical flesh of Jesus and not on the Christ consciousness in their own heart. This will keep them powerless and also prevent them from direct, open communication with heaven and Jesus. It will be a worship of the physical flesh of Jesus, which will create a false sense of salvation for the Christians and the humanity unbeknown to them. In this way, the Luciferians are in control of the earth and humanity, not Jesus and God.

Jesus wants Christians especially to understand that death on the cross provided us with forgiveness of all our sins; the physical blood that was shed on the cross does not wipe away the contamination that the sins created in your soul, but rather the spiritual blood is what performs the purification in your soul.

The spiritual blood is the sacred fire breath of the Holy Spirit and the light of Christ. It is called the baptism of the Holy Spirit and the light of Christ. It is the awakening of the divine spark of the holy Christ consciousness within the secret chamber of your heart. It is what will wipe away your sins and save you and give you eternal life. This is what the Luciferians fear the most, and they don't want you to know it. Therefore, make calls to Jesus through meditation to come into your heart to awaken the divine spark of the holy Christ consciousness or holy Christ fire. This is what Jesus wants you to do now, the time for preaching is at its peak.

Now the emphasis is on awakening of the divine man-child in your heart, the sleeping Christ in your heart, the hidden man of the heart. Your Christ consciousness is the sleeping giant in you. "Greater is he who is you, than is he who is in the world" (1 John 4:4).

Call to Jesus now and open your heart for him to come in and awaken the sleeping giant through meditation, and you will find peace and eternal life.

Jesus's Death on the Cross

Jesus's death on the cross was a demonstration to show the power of Christ consciousness in Jesus—that you cannot kill a being who has awakened his Christ consciousness. Such a being has power over death, for Christ is life, and life is Christ. Therefore when you too awaken your Christ consciousness in your heart, they will not be able to kill you, and you will never die. This is according to the hidden teachings of Jesus Christ unbeknown to many Christians.

Then how can you say he died on the cross to save you? How can a being who has power over death sacrifice his life for you? He did that by his own free will to secure you the forgiveness money to use it to pay off your dept of spiritual darkness of sin and death, which you inherited from Adam and Eve. This is the grace money— use it to pay off your dept of sin so that you might not die. Here at this stage, the Luciferian lies are exposed to set you free.

Call to Jesus Christ to come into your heart now through prayer meditation and fasting to turn on your holy Christ fire in your heart. Focus your attention on your heart. Bring your mind in tune with your heart, for your heart is the heart of God—it is the throne room of God. Here is where you meet Jesus with a stretched-forth arms, saying, "Come and sup with me. I am your elder brother. I was not sent by our Father/Mother God to earth to ask my junior brothers to worship me. No, and I say no again. I was sent here by our GodParent to awaken the divine spark of the holy Christ fire within the secret chamber of your heart which was shutdown. This is what was referred to as your spiritual fall in the Bible. And this was my mission assignment from our Parent to you on earth.

"You see, without the awakening of the Christ consciousness in your heart, you cannot make it to heaven. I, Jesus, depended upon my Christ consciousness to do the things that I did and finally made my ascension. You must awaken and depend upon your Christ consciousness in your heart. With Christ consciousness in your heart, nothing is impossible to you."

The Journey to Heaven

The journey to heaven begins from the heart of your soul. It is the awakening of the divine spark of the holy Christ fire in the heart of your soul. It is your ability to go within your soul and connect with it and use it to invite Jesus to come into your soul, body, and temple to purge you and cleanse you from all your sins, which have created the spiritual darkness in your soul.

The light of Christ, or the divine spark of fire of the Holy Spirit, will take over your soul and carry you to heaven. This is called ascension, or the rapture.

The tools to use to control and to connect with the Christ power in the heart of your soul is meditation and prayer. Your mastery of meditation and prayer is the key to complete your journey to heaven.

Jesus Wants to Meet with You

Jesus wants to meet with you personally within your temple of your soul. Your body and soul were created to be the temple of God. And the temple of God is the meeting place of God and man to do business, and Jesus wants to meet with you in your temple.

Meditation is what you used to invite him to come into your temple. Meditation is listening to God. Prayer is talking to God. Meditation is receiving energy from God and Jesus into your heart, mind, and soul. Prayer is transmitting energy from your heart, mind, body, and soul containing your desires to God and Jesus to be fulfilled.

Christ-Awakening Meditation Enters All Churches

Why is this needed? Because meditation on Christ light energy is the key to cleanse your soul from all your sins by Jesus Christ to save you from Satan and carry your soul to heaven.

The darkness of antichrist in your soul, serves as Satan's power grip to keep you in his chains on earth to pull your soul down to hell, or his underworld of darkness. That which created the darkness of antichrist in your soul were the sins you committed by Satan's temptations in your life.

Confess your faith in Christ and renounce your sins, and choose the path of righteousness to generate light in your soul to propel your soul to heaven.

The Divine Nature of Man and Woman

We were brought into life or existence by a divine family who owed their mysterious existence to themselves. They were the beginning of all things visible and invisible in the whole creation. These first mysterious beings known as Alpha and Omega gave birth to us as light beings and called us souls.

Our first habitation place was in their presence as infant souls to be nurtured by our God-Parent in the glory of God.

The main focus of the soul development was the heart and mind, the intuitive power of the heart and intellectual power of the mind. These are the two main power centers of the divine nature of man and woman. The goal of life is to develop these two power centers in your soul and use them to run your lives and be in partnership with Jesus Christ to assist God to run and expand his creation in harmony and in peace. How do you develop them? It is through meditation to connect with Jesus Christ to receive the Holy Spirit and the light of Christ into your soul on earth now to prepare you for the rapture to begin. It's an exciting time for humanity and the church.

You are learning how to take control over yourself, your soul, the spirit of God, and the light of Christ within your soul and connect with it and use it to run your eternal life in heaven.

The New and Everlasting Covenant of Jesus Christ

The new covenant means everybody must become a temple of God and a priest or priestess of his or her own temple. Paul said, "Know ye not that your body is the temple of God that the spirit of God dwells in you" (1 Corinthians 3:16). This has never been fully understood by the Christian world.

The priesthood covenant means you are breaking through the veil of spiritual darkness within your soul and make contact with the spirit of God and the light of Christ in your soul to receive divine direction pertaining to your life.

This can be done through fasting prayer and meditation to connect with Jesus Christ to receive the baptism of the Holy Spirit and the light of Christ into your soul to awaken the Christ child in the heart of your soul. The next step is to continue to use prayer and meditation to draw the Holy Spirit and the light of Christ to feed the Christ child to grow until it fills your whole soul and body.

The Holy Priesthood of Jesus Christ

He or she who can feel the Christ light in his or her heart and can see the Christ light in his or her mind is a priest or priestesses of Christ. All sons and daughters of God who have the spirit of God living in their soul body temples and can communicate with God in their temples are all priest and priestesses of God and Christ.

This priesthood is after the new and everlasting covenant as introduced by Jesus Christ to his twelve apostles at the Last Supper. It connected the old priesthood of Melchizedek to the new priesthood of the son of God together. The beginning and the end were now joined together to create balance of power and harmony and to mark the beginning of the end times—the age of the Holy Spirit, which is the homage of the divine Mother, Omega priesthood power, joining with the divine Father, Alpha priesthood power, including the priesthood power of the Son of God.

"For as many as received him, to them gave ye power to become the sons of God, as well as daughters of God." That is, anybody who received Jesus whether a man or a woman was given the power. For without this Christ light power in your soul, you cannot go to heaven. "Christ in me the hope of glory." My hope to return to the glory of God depends upon the Christ light power in the heart of my soul. Therefore, all men and women must receive this Christ-light priesthood power to be saved.

You cannot withhold this priesthood power from woman.

The Priesthood Power

The priesthood power is the main source of spiritual power to connect the human race to God through the soul. The soul is the connecting point, and the power is located in the heart of the soul and is controlled by the mind of the soul within the head.

You are a soul living in a physical body. The Christ light power is in your heart. This is the presence of God in you, and as such you are a temple of God.

You become a priest of your own temple when you are able to communicate with God in your own temple. To make it clearer, what I mean is that when you, the physical body personality, are able to link and communicate with its internal soul personality through meditation. As such, the most important thing you must do is to do nothing but to listen within through meditation and ask your soul what you should do, then follow your inner guidance. This way the guiding hands of God will direct your life into the self-mastery you seek. I call this the soul path. That means you must meditate every morning to listen to the soul voice within and follow its divine direction for everything you do, so to speak.

You must understand that as a priest of your own temple, you are responsible for the upkeep of the temple. The temple must be kept clean because every day that you meditate, the kingdom of God's light becomes brighter within you, said the Lord Jesus.

You and God are one now. You are not just an ordinary person anymore. You are God's ambassador on earth. You represent him for him to work through you. That makes you a priest of the most high God on earth. This is the key to the building of the priesthood nation, as well as the priesthood kingdom on earth.

This is the ultimate goal of Jesus and God the Creator of all things. When God is living in all things, then there is harmony and peace because he created them and all things belong to him. Yours is to learn to share with the divine Parent and assist in their divine plan as children of the holy One who hold the Christ priesthood powers on earth, which is also called Christ consciousness.

The Family

You can make your own choices by your free will, but it has to be in alignment with God's plan of Alpha and Omega to save yourself from troubles. Many people have chosen celibate life, and they have to make sure whether it is in alignment with the principles of Alpha and Omega.

Many people argue that a woman cannot hold the priesthood. They must make sure whether their argument is in accordance with the principles of Alpha and Omega, which resonates from the creative core and moved throughout the whole universe. If there is Alpha priesthood, then there should also be Omega priesthood.

Masculine priesthood, feminine priesthood, father priesthood, mother priesthood—the priesthood of God belongs to every gender, not a handful of men. Why? Because God wants to build priesthood cities of God, priesthood nations with priesthood families, to produce Christlike children to establish the kingdom of God on earth or a priesthood planet.

If God the Father will bear the title Father and God the Mother will bear the title Mother and will not produce any children, the whole universe will be empty and life will not make sense; there will be no purpose for God to create, and God will have nothing to do.

If God will produce children, then there should be a habitation for his children to live and enjoy the live their God parent has given them. This led to the creation of the universe.

Seek Empowerment from Christ First

Empowering the People of God to Become Sons and Daughters of God

> For as many as received him, to them gave the power to become the sons of God, even to them that believe on his name: Which were born, not of blood, nor of the will of the flesh, nor of the will of man, but of God. (1 John 1:12–14)

> The thief cometh not, but for to steal, and to kill, and to destroy: I am come that they might have life, and that they might have it more abundantly. (John 10:10, KJV)

> You, dear children, are from God and have overcome them, because the one who is in you is greater than the one who is in the world. (1 John 4:4, NIV)

> To whom God would make known what is the riches of the glory of this mystery among the Gentiles; which is Christ in you, the hope of glory. (Colossians 1:27, KJV)

> Then Jesus spoke to them again, saying, "I am
> the light of the world. He who follows Me shall
> not walk in darkness, but have the light of life."
> The kingdom of God is within you. (John 8:12)

The kingdom of God is hidden within the soul of man and woman. It is the blazing light of Christ that shines within the heart of the soul of man and woman. You can see it through meditation, for the pure in heart shall see Christ as light within the soul through meditation.

Discover your personal Christ power inside the heart of your soul.

Know your personal Christ and anti-Christ now

1. The Christ is the kingdom of God within you.

2. The Christ in you, is the greater is he who is in you than is he who is in the world.

3. The Christ in you the hope of glory.

4. The spirit of God that dwells in your temple is the Christ who is responsible for all your needs in life.

5. Know your personal Christ within your soul and feed him to grow brighter and brighter until the perfect day.

6. Know your personal antichrist within your soul and fight him and get rid of him from your soul.

7. Know how to sound the sacred name of Christ to generate light energy and broadcast it to purify the earth from darkness.

8. The formation of the holy army of Jesus Christ on earth to fight to defeat Satan is now.

9. Their weapon is the sounding of the sacred name of Christ to generate light to fight and cancel out the devil's spiritual darkness on earth and, if possible, stop the Armageddon.

The Full Nature of Your Being

You are a spiritual white-fire core with three sheets of bodies around it. The first sheet of body is your human physical body. The second sheet of body is your soul, and inside the soul is the spirit and the white fire core. This white-fire core is the God part of you called the Christ.

Christ in you is your personal creator who create things for you personally. He is the one who responds to your needs in your daily life. Therefore, you need to establish a strong bond with him through meditation and prayers.

You use meditation to step inside your soul temple to look inside your soul with your inner eyes, to monitor your personal light of Christ and your personal darkness of antichrist. You use meditation to connect with Jesus Christ to increase your personal light of Christ and decrease your personal darkness of antichrist within your soul temple. You use meditation to still the mind, to still the heart, and to bring your heart and mind together to join and complete the circuit, igniting it to produce a spark of light in your heart. The light in your heart is what will carry your prayers to Jesus Christ, just like how your cell phone works. You must first turn on the light in the cell phone. The light is what performs the work of transmitting your message.

Electronic Code Number

The name of Jesus Christ has electronic code number that is connected to the sound energy of his name, just like your telephone. Therefore, sounding his name will an generate energy frequency to link with your energy to communicate and to receive energy from him because both of you are connected in the same energy frequency, just like how your cell phone number works.

Man, Know Thyself

The nature of man as created by God has many level consciousness. Man has a (1) physical body, (2) soul body, (3) the spiritual body, the Christ body, and the "i am that i am" body. The last body can also be called the God body because it is the image of God in man.

The physical body is a garment or uniform with separate consciousness that is wrapped around the soul. The consciousness is what we might refer to as human consciousness or lower consciousness. Your consciousness is your awareness, becoming aware of yourself as a separate being with a sense of self.

There are five senses in the human consciousness. The sense of sight, hearing, smell, taste, and touch. These five senses give the human body the awareness to function at its level of life in the human world. It makes him a separate being with a mind capable of functioning with his own power of consciousness.

The consciousness is divided into conscious mind and the subconscious mind. The conscious mind is the messenger who is always ready to act now to fulfill your request. The subconscious mind is the messenger who stores your information in the memory bank for future use. It stores both good and evil information to be retrieved and used by the conscious mind when the need arises for the human consciousness to act.

The Soul Consciousness

The human consciousness can rise above its level and connect with the soul consciousness by opening up its sixth and seventh senses through meditation on Jesus Christ. The sixth and seventh senses are all made up of light sensors, like turning on the light bulbs for a specific wiring system in the soul and physical body to connect them together, and this can be done by Jesus Christ through meditation.

This interconnectivity of the soul can now become extensions to the light body of Christ within the soul. Herein lies the power of man and woman. This is what we might call self-realization of the spirit of God in the soul of man and woman—God in man and woman who know their own divine self, or Christ in man and woman who knows their own divine self. This is what Jesus Christ wants every Christian to reach. When you reach this level, you are now in partnership with God and Jesus Christ to run his creation.

The kingdom of God is now yours forever. You will always take a stand to defend that which is yours against Satan. This is the path that I personally have chosen, and I ask you to choose the same path. Enlightenment is the never-ending truth that comes directly from the great central light being called God to be expressed in the physical human world as divine plans from God.

Meditation

Meditation, meditation, meditation is the key.

Meditation allows us to gain access to the personal Christ within our soul. It also gives us access to Jesus Christ to invite him to come into our soul temple and request healing from him.

Meditation allows us to gain access to the planetary Christ light energy, solar Christ light energy, and the universal Christ light energy to draw into our soul. Therefore, we have enough Christ light energy to change the condition of our soul, body, and mind into Christlike nature. We can change the conditions on earth if we will learn how to draw the Christ light energy into our souls and radiate it out for healing through meditation. Jesus wants to come into our body temples, but we must meditate to invite him first.

Our Human Nature

The nature of who we are consists of two parts. The first part of ourselves is the supply part, and the second part is the need part.

The need part consists of our physical human body, which is always in need and wants so many things like food, water, clothes, and shelter, as well as cars, airplanes, ships, telephones and cell phones, to communicate, including computers, television, and etc. It also wants to build families, society cities, nations, and countries.

It is the Creator and the creative part of you that can, and has the ability to, supply you with all your needs in the form of creative concepts and ideas. The tool to use to get these creative ideas and concepts is meditation to link your lower mind of your human physical body with a higher mind of the creative parts of you in your soul. The creative supply part of you is the spirit of God and the Christ within your soul that you must depend on at all times for your needs.

Jesus said, "Draw near to God and He will draw near to you" (James 4:8, NKJV). That means draw closer to Christ within your soul, and Christ within your soul will draw closer to you to give you everything you need in the form of creative ideas and concepts to apply to get what you want. You must do this through meditation to establish the spiritual link between your two natures.

This is what constitutes the priesthood—the ability to use meditation and prayer to go within your soul temple to communicate with God and Christ to receive your needs. Those who have specialized in prophecies have become spokesmen of disaster as well as blessings from God.

Connecting Point

The heart of your soul is the connecting point to heaven, God, and Jesus Christ. In order to see and communicate with heaven, God, and Jesus Christ, you must look through the heart of your soul with your attention focused on Christ within you. This process is called meditation.

In the secret chamber of your heart is the holy Christ fire to link you to heaven and Jesus. At this point in time, you have become a high priest of your own body and soul temple because you can now enter into your temple at will through meditation.

Empowering the people of God to become sons and daughters of God

> For as many as received him, to them gave the power to become the sons of God, even to them that believe on his name: Which were born, not of blood, nor of the will of the flesh, nor of the will of man, but of God. (1 John 1:12–14, KJV)

> The thief cometh not, but for to steal, and to kill, and to destroy: I am come that they might have life, and that they might have it more abundantly. (John 10:10, KJV)

You, dear children, are from God and have overcome them, because the one who is in you is greater than the one who is in the world. (1 John 4:4, NIV)

To whom God would make known what is the riches of the glory of this mystery among the Gentiles; which is Christ in you, the hope of glory. (Colossians 1:27, KJV)

Then Jesus spoke to them again, saying, "I am the light of the world. He who follows Me shall not walk in darkness, but have the light of life." (John 8:12, NKJV))

The kingdom of God is within you. The kingdom of God is hidden within the soul of man and woman. It is the blazing light of Christ that shines within the heart of the soul of man and woman, and you can see it through meditation. For the pure in heart shall see Christ as light within the soul through meditation.

1. This is the kingdom of God within you.

2. This is the greater is he who is in you than is he who is in the world.

3. This is the Christ in you the hope of glory.

4. This is the spirit of God that dwells in your temple whose responsibility is to respond to all your needs in life.

5. Know your personal Christ within your soul, and feed him to grow brighter and brighter until the perfect day.

6. Know your personal antichrist within your soul, and fight him and get rid of him from your soul,

7. Know how to sound the sacred name of Christ to generate light energy and broadcast it to purify the earth from darkness.

8. The formation of the holy army of Jesus Christ on earth to fight to defeat Satan is now.

9. Their weapon is the sounding of the sacred name of Christ to generate light to fight and cancel out the devil's spiritual darkness on earth and, if possible, stop the Armageddon.

The Full Nature of Your Being

You are a spiritual white-fire core with three sheets of bodies around it. The first sheet of body is your human physical body. The second sheet of body is your soul, and inside the soul is the spirit and the white fire core. This white-fire core is the God part of you called the Christ and has Christ consciousness.

Christ in you is your personal creator who create things for you personally. He is the one who responds to all your needs in your daily life. Therefore, you need to establish a strong bond with him through meditation and prayers. "I do all things in Christ who strengthens me." You use meditation to step inside your soul temple to look inside your soul with your inner eyes, to monitor your personal light of Christ and your personal darkness of antichrist. You use meditation to increase your personal light of Christ and decrease your personal darkness of antichrist within your soul temple through grace and works of righteousness.

You use meditation to still the mind, to still your heart, and to bring your heart and mind together, igniting to produce a spark of light in your heart. "Be still and know that I am God."

The light in your heart is what will carry your prayers to Jesus Christ, just like how your cell phone works. You must first turn on the light in the cell phone. The light is what performs the work of transmitting your message.

The name Jesus Christ has an electronic code-number frequency. The sound of the name Jesus Christ has an electronic code number frequency connected to the sound energy of his name, just like your telephone number. Therefore, sounding his name will generate an energy frequency to link with your energy to communicate and to receive energy from him because both of you are connected in the same energy frequency, just like how your cell phone number works. These are some of the hidden teaching that Jesus Christ gave to his apostles to use to spiritually communicate with him.

Call his name every day for your Christ-consciousness empowerment, my beloved brothers and sisters.

Can the Creator Hide Himself from His Creation?

No matter what we do in life, a time will come when we will stand face to face with the Creator of us all. Can the Creator hide himself from his creation or vice versa? The Creator loves his creation; therefore, he will try to save everything that he has created.

We read from the Bible that one of his creations, man, fell spiritually from his presence and a rescue attempt had to be designed and be implemented to save man and earth.

The requirements to live in heaven are Christ body, Christ blood, and Christ consciousness. The requirements to live on earth, or the human world, is human body, human blood, and human consciousness. Your soul has to be clothed with one of these requirements to qualify to enter one of these worlds.

Then the question is, how can this be achieved?. This is where Jesus comes in with a plan from heaven to address this needs. The Bible says in John 1:12–13, "For as many as received him, to them gave ye power to become the sons of God, even to them that were born, not of blood, nor of the will of the flesh, nor of the will of man, but of God."

What kind of souls do we have on earth today?

We have two groups of souls on the planet today. First are the souls that are spiritually awakened, and second are the souls that are spiritually asleep; that is, unawakened souls.

What are these spiritually asleep and spiritually awakened souls?

The soul that is spiritually asleep means that the spiritual light in the heart of the soul is not awakened yet by Jesus Christ through the fire baptism of the heart. Therefore, there is a spiritual darkness in that soul—the soul is in the dark night or sleep state. The spiritually awakened state of the soul is where the spiritual light in the heart of the soul is awakened to produce spiritual light to push out the spiritual darkness to bring in the daytime.

The daytime is when we all wake up from sleep. The nighttime is when we all fall asleep. At this time on earth, we are now in the time of spiritual-light awakening of the soul by Jesus Christ.

A Planet of Families and Eternal Family

Life is based upon the eternal family life. God is the supreme family of the universe, and we are the reflection of his life system and his agenda on our planet. Why? Because we didn't create ourselves and the planet we live on today. Everything was created by God for his purposes, and his purpose was to bless us to serve his purpose.

We are the offspring and the handiwork of God; we have his image and likeness. We are here to express his divine will on this planetary earthly kingdom he has given to us. His goal for us is to live in peace, love, and harmony and also to expand; that is, to take dominion over the earth and be fruitful in his universal kingdom. We are to progress and become like Jesus Christ to give us the ability to go to heaven and to travel to other celestial planetary kingdoms in the holy light universe or the glory of God.

This is our supreme destiny as ordained by our God-Parent. Whether we believe it or not, you can't change it. You can accept these blessings and enjoy it, or you can refuse it and join Satan's kingdom. The choice is yours, for blessings cannot be forced upon a person. One must discover for himself what he wants his life to be in order to appreciate it, then his life would be worth living, and he would continue living in the eternal world.

Satan was once living in heaven and rebelled against God because he didn't appreciate his life in heaven. God doesn't want anyone to come to heaven and later on change his mind and rebel against him. This is unacceptable because it will create havoc and heaven will cease to be peaceful and will be unpleasant to live in eternity.

In order to live in heaven as a family, you must learn to abide by the heavenly family rules or laws. For that which is governed by law is also preserved by law, for there is no kingdom in which there is no law to preserve it. Satan disobeyed God's law and fell spiritually to hell.

Our Earth Family Life

Our earth family life is a training ground to prepare us to inherit eternal family life. Initially, in the garden of Eden, God said it was not good for man to be alone. Now if it is not good for man to be alone, then how would it be good for God to be alone in heaven? So God created for Adam a female to form the first family union on earth.

This is the supreme eternal family themselves speaking. God said, "Let us create man in our image." In the image of God created them, male and female. Therefore, the image God is Father/Mother God (Alpha and Omega). This is their supreme eternal agenda for us as sons and daughters of God on earth—making love and producing children is part of the divine plan.

God is the supreme eternal family in heaven and of the holy light universe. We are to exemplify his life on earth as sons and daughters of God. That means we too must build families as designed by God the Creator. He said, "I am Alpha and Omega," meaning masculine and feminine being, the Father/Mother God who gave birth to the first Christ and us, sons and daughters of God.

We are here on earth to express the will of our God-Parent as exemplified by Jesus Christ to us—to learn to become masters of love and receive the power of Christ consciousness, which we have lost through the spiritual fall of Adam and Eve, and then return to our celestial home with our holy Christed families and live there forever with Jesus Christ and our God-Parent.

About the Author

John Entsuah was born in Ghana, West Africa. He came to United State in 1974. John has a beautiful wife and five wonderful children. He has studied religion at Summit University at Malibu, California, where he learned more about the nature of God, Jesus the Christ, the universe and creation, as well as the origin of man.

John has many occupations including maintenance technician, refrigeration technician, maintenance engineer at Ablestick adhesive plant in Los Angeles California, electrician on merchant marine ships

U.S Navy ships, as well as worked on air conditioners and steam boilers.

For over forty years, John has had personal, spiritual experiences that have enriched his life and motivated him to research into man's purpose in life. It is these things that have inspired, motivated, and compelled him to research into man's purpose in life. It is these things that have inspired, motivated and compelled him to write this book.

He himself has had to wrestle with who God really is, learn about the relationship with Jesus the Christ, develop an understanding about the nature of the universe and heaven, and examine man's spiritual fall, as well as how to return to his former state of existence. John's purpose for writing this book is the hope that the Christians will eventually learn how to combine their prayer with meditation and fasting to connect directly with Jesus Christ himself spiritually, to receive the atonement power of the Holy Spirit and the light of Christ in the heart of their souls as the grace to be born again into sons and daughters of God, with Christ body, Christ blood and Christ consciousness to enter into the kingdom of God.

He strongly believes that Christ consciousness is the only hope for the human race.

Apostle Paul said. "If any man be in Christ, he is a new creature. Old things are passed away, behold all things are become new." (2 Corinthians 5:17).

CHRIST AWAKENING AGE MINISTRY

13370 CLEAR CANYON CT EASTVALE, CA 92880

John Entsuah

Christ awakening gospel teacher.
christcome@aol.com

christ awakening meditation prayer christawakening.org

www.ingramcontent.com/pod-product-compliance
Lightning Source LLC
Chambersburg PA
CBHW051229120626
46547CB00013B/1573